Budget Alert

FISCAL POLICY ISSUES IN GRENADA

Laurel Theresa Bain

Acknowledgement

Budget Alert originated from the Fiscal Alert production of the Bain's Sisters that was hosted by the late George Grant. On the publication of this first series of Budget Alert, the Bain Sisters acknowledge the life and contribution of the veteran journalist George Grant to national development, fand specifically the use of his broadcasting skills and medium to facilitate dialogue on the issues touching and concerning the citizens of Grenada.

Fiscal Alert with the Bain Sisters – Laurel Bain, Gemma Bain-Thomas, and Dr. Janice Bain used the platform of George Grant's Grenada Broadcast to air a weekly programme which commenced in October 2019 and continued until March 2020. George facilitated the programme every Monday morning on his "Gudday Grenada".

Fiscal Alert was a new addition to his broadcasting, and we reveled in sharing knowledge and experience on fiscal policies and other economic and social issues. George was happy to accommodate Fiscal Alert, as in his own words, "the programme was an eye opener". Initially, we agreed on a twenty-minute feature; but many times, were accommodated beyond the time allotted.

The Bain Sisters bonded quickly with George. His matter of fact but easy going way of doing things filtered through. We looked forward to and were ready every Monday morning for Fiscal Alert in keeping with the theme, "Knowledge is Power, and

Experience is the Greatest Teacher". George embraced Fiscal Alert as it sought to bring the business of government closer to the people by improving their understanding of government policies and measures in a straightforward and simple manner.

The Fiscal Alert Team is indebted to George for the use of his platform; and for giving us the opportunity and a forum to engage and educate the citizens of Grenada on economic and social issues.

The last communication between the Bain's Sisters and George Grant was on April 25th, 2020, when we shared information with him of Dr. Janice Bain's activities on the frontline in fighting the Covid-19 in the USA. In his unique way, George commended her for her service. We are thankful to George for his service and contribution to national development. Budget Alert emanated from the engagement with George Grant to whom this Budget Alert is dedicated.

Table of Contents

Budget Alert is a series of Articles on economic and fiscal issues in Grenada, emanating from the national budgets. In Grenada, and in the other countries of the Eastern Caribbean Currency Union (ECCU), fiscal policy is the main instrument for managing the economy.[1] Fiscal policy is generally pursued through the implementation of the national budget.

The national budget is described as the financial plan for the country. Ideally, the first step in the preparation of the national budget is a determination of the available financial resources which are domestic revenue, grants, and loans. These financial resources are then allocated among competing expenditure items namely salaries, wages, goods, services, transfers, and subsidies which are necessary for Government to undertake its operations. Financial resources are also channeled into Government capital projects, net lending and to debt repayments. The details of the budget are presented in the Estimates of Revenue and Expenditure. The Appropriation Bill, which

---

1   The countries of the Eastern Caribbean Currency Union are:

Anguilla, Antigua and Barbuda, The Commonwealth of Dominica, Grenada, Montserrat, St Kitts and Nevis, Saint Lucia, and St Vincent and the Grenadines.

They are members of the organization of Eastern Caribbean States (OECS) which was established by the Treaty of Basseterre in 1981. They currently operate under the Revised Treaty of Basseterre of 2010. The countries are members of the Eastern Caribbean Central Bank. which was established by the Eastern Caribbean Central Bank (ECCB) Agreement of 1983 as a common Central Bank to serve these countries. The countries are also members of Caricom.

is approved by Parliament for expenditure for a particular purpose during a financial year, is the legal document that accompanies the Estimates of Revenue and Expenditure.

Budget Alert highlights some of the economic and fiscal issues from the 2021 National Budget in a series of Articles. It commences with proposals for transforming Grenada's economy, and includes proposals for the 2021 and 2022 national budgets. Among the Articles are issues related to the national debt; the repurchase of the WRB shares in the Grenada Electricity Services Company (GRENLEC); the status of Government finances; and the reform of the Fiscal Responsibility Act. Budgeting is a continuous process and issues in one fiscal year inform the policies and programmes that would be outlined in the next national budget.

Budget Alert is a reliable and credible source of information on issues arising from the national budgets. See Appendix 1 with the dates of the publication of the Budget Alert articles in 2021.

Transforming the Economy

Proposals for the 2021 National Budget

It is budget time again. It will be the 2021 National Budget. The public eagerly awaits the Budget Speech, as delivered by the Minister for Finance, detailing government's policies, and programmes for the economic and social transformation of Grenada. At the pinnacle of the budget presentation would be the strategy for protecting the health of the nation. The Budget Speech will obviously be the most visible. The other important documents would be the Estimates of Revenue and Expenditure and the Appropriation Bill.

On Budget Day, the public will be informed of how the government intends to raise revenue to finance its expenditure for 2021. The Budget Speech will provide information on government's priorities for 2021 and its taxation policy. The action of the government to raise revenue and the direction of its spending will impact on all in the economy, either as individuals, households, businesses, and both government and non-government organisations.

The finalisation of the 2021 budget should be at an advanced stage. The Finance Committee of Parliament, based on the Public Finance Management Act, should as of 1st November 2020 be thoroughly examining the estimates of Revenue and Expenditure for 2021. The Finance Committee by then should have the Medium-Term Debt Management Strategy (2021 – 2023) which provides a comprehensive analysis of the public sector debt, the risks inherent in the debt and the Government's strategy for mitigating the risks.

In this Covid-19 recessionary environment, what are the expectations for the 2021 National Budget? Fundamental to the presentation of the Budget is a comprehensive assessment of the current and forecasted economic and social conditions. The Covid-19 crisis has resulted in a steep decline in GDP and in serious social dislocation particularly in the areas of employment, education, and many social activities. The result of this assessment will determine the priorities for the 2021 Budget and in the medium term.

The focus of the 2021 National Budget should be on stabilising the economy, addressing the issues of the vulnerable groups and economic recovery. While doing this, government should also be remodelling the pillars for transforming the economy by undertaking a thorough and critical examination of the National Sustainable Development Plan.

In stabilising the economy, a primary focus should be on halting further decline in incomes and by extension GDP. However, while addressing the decline in incomes, the stabilisation of the economy should be extended to the social sectors particularly education and health. The education sector has been displaced, the health services inadequate and the informal sector has been left in distress. The stabilisation programme must be well integrated with the recovery strategy.

The recovery strategy should immediately focus on increasing employment and reducing imports (which are foreign exchange leakages) by consciously developing the agriculture sector, inclusive of livestock and fishing. This should be combined with supporting and encouraging cottage type agro-processing which could be undertaken in small facilities. However, the objective should be to reduce the import bill while generating employment. This will allow for the informal sector and other vulnerable groups to be integrated in the recovery strategy. The 2021 National Budget should indicate the technical and financial support, and any incentives that will be provided to facilitate the development of a technologically driven agricultural sector and the accompanying agro-processing. On the marketing side, is there a role for a transformed National Marketing and Importing Board? An output from the budget should therefore be a well-designed development package for agriculture, inclusive of livestock and fishing.

As a small an open economy, there is a need to earn foreign exchange. Therefore, Grenada needs to produce goods and services for export. There could be scope for the export of non-tourism services. Professional services such as legal, medical, accounting, tutoring, culture, web design and data analysis could be exported virtually. The legislative and administrative requirements to access external markets should be investigated. The government could, through its overseas missions, facilitate the export of these professional services. These could be promoted to reduce the high dependence on tourism.

In stabilising the education and health sectors, structures and systems that would transform the economy should be established. Immediate attention should be given to the students that may be dropping out of the education system due to the Covid-19 related approaches to teaching. The issue of equitable access to education outside of a classroom setting must be a priority to avoid worsening the long-term outcomes for already disadvantaged groups.

The budget must also address the need for a remodelling of the community health centres with the objective of reducing the demands on the General Hospital. A blend of telemedicine and physical medical attention along with a widening of the range of services will need to be considered. A pronouncement on the National Health Insurance would need to be included in the budget as the consultative process began in 2020

The budget will also need to focus on protecting the environment and developing the infrastructure of the country including the electronic infrastructure. It would be an appropriate time to provide information to the public on the impact, economic, environmental, and social, of the large tourism projects in Levera and Mt. Hartman and their consistency with the National Sustainable Development Plan.

The financial resources to facilitate the economic recovery will extend beyond the government. However, along with its direct responsibility for financing the budget, the government should include in the budget any policies of the financial institution for supporting the recovery process.

The financing of the 2021 Budget will need to be presented with clarity. Domestic revenue for 2020 will be substantially reduced when compared with the budgeted amount. Domestic revenue is not expected to increase significantly in 2021. If grants are available these should be readily utilised. For the 2021 Budget, consideration should be given to renegotiating the alternative use of grants to deserving areas in light of the Covid-19 crisis. However, inflows of grants along with the domestic revenue will not be adequate to finance government's total fiscal operations in 2021; inclusive of the required repayment of principal on debt. The government will therefore need to seek financing for the 2021 National Budget.

The first area to be tapped for financing is the reserves, that is, savings from previous budgets. Are there such available resources? Additionally, the budget should state how the resources from the National Transformation Fund will be used to finance the stabilisation and recovery strategy. Contracting new debt to finance government operations in 2021 should be a last resort; but this will be the ultimate if there are no alternative sources of financing. Contracting debt will most likely be the option available to the government. A resort to debt financing has implications for the debt to GDP ratio, which in this Covid-19 recessionary environment, is already higher than the targeted fifty-five (55) percent of GDP.

In this context, a pronouncement will need to be made on the fiscal policy framework and the Medium-term Fiscal Framework. In addressing the policy framework, the Minister for Finance should provide information on whether the budget for 2021 is guided by the Fiscal Responsibility Act. The fiscal rules and targets were suspended in March 2020 for one fiscal year. With the suspension of the rules and targets, the Fiscal Responsibility Act makes provision for a Recovery Plan Memorandum to be submitted to Parliament. The Budget will need to outline the content of the Recovery Plan Memorandum and indicate whether the suspension of the rules and targets is extended to 2021.

The Covid-19 crisis has provided opportunities. It is therefore an appropriate time to examine the Fiscal responsibility Act for its consistency and transparency and as a policy instrument to facilitate economic development and transformation. With protecting the health of the nation at the pinnacle, a well-integrated economic stabilization and recovery strategy should be the focus of the 2021 National Budget. This strategy must be consistent with plans for developing and transforming the economy.

Covid-19 Induced Approach to Transforming the Economy – Resetting the National Sustainable Development Plan (NSDP).

The lessons learnt from the Covid-19 global crisis should be used as the basis for charting the way forward and transforming the local economy. A previous article on 'Reflections from the Covid-19 Global Crisis' highlighted that: 1. Globalization is real, facilitated by the integration of economies through Travel, Investment and Trade (TIT) and technological platforms that allow for instant communication. 2. Regional integration was left wanting, due to a lack of a common and coherent strategy to address the Covid-19 crisis. 3 Significant shortcomings in the economic models of development emerged as a result of the heavy reliance on inflows from tourism, financial services, and the Citizen by Investment (CBI) programmes. 4. The informal sector landed in 'no man's land' as many of the participants in that sector fell through a crack when policies were developed to address the impact of the Covid-19 crisis. 5. Inclusiveness in nation building needs to be more than pronouncements as institutional arrangements were either non-existent, non-operational, or ad hoc. 6 Technological enhancements must be accompanied with deeper technological penetration to cater for persons without access; and 7. Preparedness for disaster should be enhanced by adopting an all-hazard strategy.

These issues should now inform a resetting of the National Sustainable Development Plan (NSDP). The NSDP, as laid in Parliament on 20 November 2019, is broad based and informative. However, it needs to be more strategic and integrated. A resetting of the NSDP is necessary due to the existing Covid-19 environment. In the resetting, the strong and steady pillars of the NSDP must be placed in the international and regional context. International treaties and regulations that will influence national policies and programmes should be included with clarity.

Importantly, with globalization, the small economies of the Eastern Caribbean Currency Union (ECCU) must be positioned to operate in the global economy and to be resilient to shocks. This could only be achieved through strong regional integration. A component of resetting the NSDP will be introspections and approaches to incorporating policies and programmes that could be better implemented through regional cooperation. The revised Treaty of Basseterre, which established the OECS Economic Union, has significant implications for cooperation and this should be maximized. Due to the small size of the individual economies of the ECCU, transformation of the economies could only be achieved through cooperation within the regional integration framework.

In this introspection and approaches to regional integration, the priority must be given to balancing international policies, particularly trade policies, with the resilience of the national economies. This also requires a rethinking of the models of development for these economies, which cannot be too bias towards the adoption of competitive international trade policies and a high dependence on tourism. During the crisis, countries focused on the resilience of their domestic economy. For the small countries of the Eastern Caribbean Currency Union (ECCU), the resilience of the domestic economy should be addressed in its regional context. Within that framework, the NSDP should include a strategic and clear policy on the sectors that will be allowed to compete internationally and those that will be supported to ensure the resilience of the economy. This has implications for the development of the agriculture sector, manufacturing, and agro-processing. It is important for the strategy for national resilience to be anchored in the regional context as most trade agreements are negotiated on a regional basis.

Another critical component of the NSDP that should be anchored in the regional context is technological enhancement and deeper technological penetration. With the dependence on technology for all aspects of life, access to technology is appropriately described as a public good, requiring universal access. However, with a focus on national resilience, the vulnerabilities of such dependence must be considered. The regional integration context must include programmes for reducing the cost of government while improving the efficiency in the production and delivery of goods and services. Areas that could be targeted for regional cooperation are health, education, security, agriculture, manufacturing, and tourism.

The function and nature of the financial sector, for ease of access to finance, must also be addressed within the regional framework. This is critical for the countries of the ECCU that share a common Central Bank and monetary arrangement.

The international and regional context is a necessary component in resetting the NSDP. The synchronizing of the regional and national policies for transforming the domestic economy will be guided by a conscious policy to develop self-sufficiency in critical sectors. The transformed economy will be manifested by the radical changes in the social sectors particularly education and health and the economic sectors of agriculture, manufacturing, and tourism. The integration of these productive sectors while protecting the environment; and the supportive role of the education sector is important in transforming the economy.

The professional services sector should be developed, not only to serve the demands of the domestic economy but also to export these services.

A resetting of the National Sustainable Development Plan in the international and regional context, while strengthening the domestic economy, is needed for the transformation of Grenada's economy.

Reflections on the Covid-19 Pandemic

Without reflection, we go blindly on our way, creating more unintended consequences, and failing to achieve anything useful. Margaret J. Wheatley

The Covid-19 pandemic is being described as fighting a war against an invisible enemy. The war is lethal in terms of lives lost; and is having a severe impact on the economies. After each battle, it is necessary to debrief, to undertake an assessment of the status quo in preparation for the next battle.

The pandemic continues and is destroying both lives and livelihood. In 2020, incomes were drastically reduced and are likely to be further reduced in 2021 with the associated elevated unemployment and poverty. With over sixty (60) Covid related deaths and the rapid spread of the virus to over two thousand, six hundred (2,600) persons within one month, both lives and livelihood are being lost. It is therefore necessary to address both lives and livelihood simultaneously. They cannot be separated.

Following the initial phase of the Covid-19 battle which commenced in March 2020, there was adequate time to reflect and prepare for the onslaught of the next phase of August 2021. While attention is now placed on aggressively protecting lives and livelihood, there must be an element of reflection as a basis for charting the way forward. The following is extracted, in part, from a previously published article entitled 'Reflections from the Covid-19 Global Crisis'. This is applicable in addressing the second phase of the pandemic while charting the way forward. On reflection it is obvious that:

Globalization is not only a concept; it is real. The integration of the economies through trade, investment, and travel (TIT) was vividly manifested. All aspects of the impact of Covid-19 were transmitted globally. This was further facilitated by instant electronic communication. Electronic communication platforms allowed for the real time transmission of information which required the synchronization of information sharing. This proved to be an impossible task.

Regional integration was left wanting when it was most needed. Regional integration arrangements were established as early as 1965, with the Caribbean Free Trade Agreement (CARIFTA), to assist small Caribbean economies to be competitive through trade facilitation. The integration process was further strengthened in 1973 with the establishment of CARICOM to support the development of its member countries. Recognizing their extreme vulnerability. the OECS Economic Union was established in 2010 for the harmonization of policies and the free movement of labour and capital in the Eastern Caribbean Currency Union.

The principles of regional integration were not practiced during the crisis. This was manifested in the absence of a coherent and common approach for treating with the Covid-19 crisis. It was visible in the different approaches adopted by countries to tourism, and in particular, the cruise ship industry. The resolving of the issues between Barbados and Trinidad and Tobago on the treatment of travelling Trinidad and Tobago nationals; and the exchanges between Grenada and St Vincent and the Grenadines on trading in the Grenadines during the crisis are instructive. Regionalism may have worked with respect to procurement of health supplies and with regional testing to some extent but overall, a lot more is desired.

Significant shortcomings in the present economic models of development have emerged. A major indictment of this model is the proportion of the population without savings to sustain them for short periods without income, coupled with their lack of access to social security benefits, inadequate health services and substandard housing and other living conditions. The economic models of development need to be revisited. In the Eastern Caribbean Currency Union (ECCU), the economies are heavily dependent on tourism, which is known to be vulnerable to external shocks. The other main sectors or sources of financial inflows are financial services and citizenship by investment or the sale of passport. Construction activity is also related to these financial inflows. The economies are therefore severely impacted by the Covid-19 Pandemic.

While this recession is unique, it highlights the need to strike a balance between inward and outward looking strategies; and to carefully scrutinize policies of trade liberalization and other internationally synchronized policies.

The informal sector landed in "no man's land." In all the economies of the ECCU, there is an important, informal sector whose contribution to national output is unknown. Many of the numerous players in this informal sector are not registered in the institutional system such as the financial institutions, national insurance schemes, private insurance, and/or government departments or agencies. They fall through a wide crack when addressing the impact of the crisis. Other vulnerable groups, though not included in the informal sector, are the poor, elderly, and the physically and mentally challenged who are also falling into the crack.

Inclusiveness in nation building *needs* to be more than pronouncements. The pillars of good governance seem to be shaky. Institutional arrangements for inclusiveness in times of a national crisis appeared to be either non-existent, non-operational, or ad hoc. It is critical that genuine concern for each citizen be displayed during normal times, and this will make it easier for citizens to bind together during crisis.

Preparedness for disasters ought to be enhanced. The countries of the ECCU are frequently impacted by tropical storms and hurricanes which have resulted in the destruction of economic and social assets, and loss of lives. International and regional agencies are working with Member States in preparing national disaster plans and the establishment of disaster response agencies. The focus of these plans has been on climate related disasters. Epidemics, although occurring frequently, are generally excluded. The scope of disaster planning and preparedness must be broadened, incorporating an all-hazard strategy.

It is important for technological advancement to be accompanied with deeper technological penetration. The current widespread use of electronic communication for all aspects of life has essentially excluded members of the population without such access. This has implications for their participation in, among other things, commerce, and education.

It is undoubtable that a new economy is in the making. A reflection on the experiences will inform the path to the transformation of the economies of the Eastern Caribbean Currency Union (ECCU) and Grenada in particular.

A Budget With a Human Touch

It would be time for the presentation of the National Budget for 2022. The public would be informed of the policies and programs for 2022, the expenditures associated with these and the sources of financing for the expenditures. The economic, social, and budgetary developments in 2021 should inform the policies and programmes for the 2022 National Budget.

The 2021 Budget was presented with optimism under the theme Recovery, Transformation and Resilience. The theme was appropriate as the economy declined sharply by 14 percent in 2020 due to the Covid-19 Pandemic. The projected growth rate of 6 percent for 2021 was based on an estimated expansion in economic activity associated with the easing of the Covid-19 Pandemic; and the aggressive implementation of the Central Government capital programme. The persistence of the Covid-19 Pandemic and the controversies on fiscal matters overshadowed the implementation of the 2021 National Budget.

The emergence of a Covid cluster in December 2020 downgraded the prospects of achieving the projected 6 percent economic growth for 2021. The tourism industry remains subdued. The reopening of the St Georges University in August had the potential of boosting the economy. However, in that same month, the Covid-19 Pandemic intensified rapidly with the associated negative effects on the economy. The prospect of achieving economic growth in 2021 is slim. The sluggish economy was accompanied with higher prices. This has resulted in a decline in real income thereby reducing the amount of goods and services that could be purchased with existing incomes. It could be deduced that unemployment and poverty remained elevated in 2021. It is therefore a harsh economic period for economic agents, particularly for the vulnerable groups.

The state of Government finances, as of June 2021, was published in the article on 'Government Finances and the Economy Part 3'. With the spread of Covid-19 infections from August and the associated negative economic and social impacts, improvements in the Government finances are not expected in the second half of the year. Consequently, the growth in public debt would persist in 2021. Beyond the published data, there were critical fiscal issues being addressed. Foremost among these were the repurchase of the WRB shares in GRENLEC by the Government; payment of the 4 percent increase of salary to public officers; payment of outstanding Court awarded judgement debts; status of pension and gratuity for public officers; and issues of fiscal transparency associated with the comprehensiveness of the fiscal reports. It is in this context that the 2022 National Budget would be presented.

The 2022 Budget is expected to be guided by the Fiscal Responsibility Act. The Resolution was passed in Parliament, in March 2021, to suspend the fiscal rules and targets for the 2021 fiscal year. A Recovery Plan Memorandum was prepared with the measures to be implemented to ensure compliance with the fiscal rules and targets at the end of the suspension period. The Fiscal Responsibility Act (2015) would therefore be in effect for the 2022 fiscal year unless it is amended or repealed.

The theme of the Budget adopted for 2021 of Recovery, Transformation and Resilience is still relevant for 2022 as the economy remains depressed. However, there is the need to directly address the social fall-out associated with the Pandemic and the high unemployment and poverty. In the already harsh economic conditions, it is important that the theme of the 2022 National Budget include the phrase 'With a Human Touch'. This will allow for the decisions, policies and programmes that are implemented to include elements that alleviate the suffering of the vulnerable groups.

In this context, poverty and unemployment should be addressed frontally. The focus on the human element would eliminate the State pushing citizens into poverty through its approach to the settlement of rightfully due financial obligations. In the current difficult economic period, the cost of continuous impasse between Government and citizens, has not only been detrimental to affected individuals and their families, but has placed additional financial burden on the entire population.

A Budget with a human touch would also focus on strengthening the education system and the health sector. In strengthening the education system, urgent attention would need to be given to the students that may be dropping out or lagging due to the Covid-19 related approaches to teaching. The Covid-19 Pandemic has vividly demonstrated the need for an overhaul of the health system, inclusive of its integration with the proposed National Health Insurance. A focus on these social areas would be consistent with a National Budget with a human touch. Development is about people and their quality of life. If the wellbeing of the citizens is not placed at the forefront of policies, society would disintegrate and there would be no development.

The economic or structural policies to be pursued as the economy recovers from the Covid-19 Pandemic have been outlined in the previous article on "Proposals for the 2021 National Budget". The fundamentals of the economy have not changed and the proposals remain relevant. Given the persistence of depressed economic activity, more aggressive fiscal policy must be pursued in 2022. Fiscal policy should aim at achieving growth but should also be targeted at alleviating the plight of the vulnerable groups. In periods of economic recession, Government fiscal policy should be to reduce taxes, and/or increase expenditure. This should be the policy approach to the 2022 National Budget.

The revenue system should be thoroughly examined to identify areas for relief. Grenada's current or operational revenue is dominated by tax revenue. As of June 2021, current or operational revenue amounted to $352.1M of which $304M or 86.3 percent was tax revenue. Grenada's tax revenue is derived mainly from indirect or expenditure related taxes which amounted to $219.5M or 72.2 percent of the tax revenue, comprising mainly of import duty and Value Added Tax (VAT). The revenue yield from these expenditure-related taxes has increased during the first half of 2021 due to, in part, the higher values on which the taxes are applied (the tax base) associated with global inflation and increases in freight rates.

Specifically, import duty and the customs service charge are applied on the value of the imported goods, inclusive of the cost of the good and the insurance and freight (CIF). Therefore, higher international prices and freight rates are automatically transmitted into higher tax revenue. The revenue yield from the VAT is influenced twice from global inflation and higher freight rate. The VAT is a tax on domestic consumption or local purchases of goods and services. Therefore, the value on which VAT is applied comprises the CIF in addition to the calculated import duty and the customs service charge which already include elements of the higher international prices and freight rate. Further, if the goods and services are then sold by internal marketing outlets, unless the product is exempt from VAT or zero rated, the domestic prices become another component of the tax base. With the higher freight and prices, Government coffers have benefited from the higher value of goods and services. This is good for the Government finances particularly during this period of slow economic growth. However, it places a greater tax burden on the low income workers, unemployed, poor, and other vulnerable groups particularly during a period of rising prices. Policy measures to reduce the tax burden and direct levies and fees particularly on these vulnerable groups should be a feature of the 2022 National Budget.

Government expenditure policies should aim at improving the effectiveness and efficiency of expenditure, with an immediate focus on goods and services and transfers and subsidies. In this new economic environment, the modes of delivery of public services have changed and the opportunity should be taken to reform the delivery of goods and services to reduce unit cost and improve efficiency. The transfers and subsidies component of Government expenditure, which is dominated by allocations to social safety net programmes, while providing well targeted income support should aim at elevating persons out of poverty and supporting a transformed economy.

The 2022 National Budget should present a well packaged and realistic capital programme based on the need to restructure the economy. The persistence of the Covid-19 pandemic globally requires a rethinking of the approach to tourism. The capital budget should highlight programmes for accelerating the development of the agriculture sector and agro-processing; strengthening the provision of professional and creative services; and transforming the education and health sectors. The path towards the transformation of Grenada's economy should be the most prominent feature of the capital programme for 2022.

The availability of fiscal reserves and the financial status of the National Transformation Fund would determine to what extent these could be sources of financing for the 2022 National Budget. These should be the first financing options and their role in financing the budget should be explicit and transparent. A cautious approach to contracting new debt should be adopted and should be the last resort.

The public would eagerly await the Budget Speech which continues to be the most visible and attention grabbing. However, this should not distract the public from thoroughly examining the legally binding Estimates of Revenue and Expenditure and accompanying documents such as The Medium-term Debt Strategy, the Borrowing Plan, and the Medium-term Fiscal Framework.

Analysis of the 2022 National Budget – Part 1

The National Budget for 2022 would contribute to economic growth mainly through the provisions for increased expenditure. Rightfully so, as during a recession, the objective of fiscal policy is to resuscitate economic activity. This is achieved through reduction in taxes or/and increased expenditure. The accompanying higher disposable income is expected to increase spending for both consumption and investment purposes, resulting in an expansion in economic output and national income. It is generally anticipated that the higher economic growth would lead to reduced unemployment and poverty.

The 2022 National Budget is analyzed in two parts. A review of the legislative framework and the economic and social context of the Budget is undertaken in this article [Part 1]. The budget proposals and their implications for the economy are examined in the next article [Part 2].

The Legislative Framework

The budgetary process is governed by [i] The Constitution, [ii] The Public Finance Management Act, [iii] The Debt Management Act, [iv] the Fiscal Responsibility Act, and [v] the Audit Act.

Consistent with the Constitution, and a good practice, the Budget was presented before the

beginning of the fiscal year. The presentation of the budget statement was accompanied with the laying of the Appropriation Bill and the Estimates of Revenue and Expenditure before Parliament. Contrary to the legislative requirement, some documents were not presented to Parliament by the time of the budget.

In the budget statement, the Minister of Finance advised that the following reports would be submitted to Parliament namely: the Medium-term Fiscal Framework, the Fiscal Risk Statement, the Medium-term Debt Strategy, and the Annual Debt Report. The Annual Borrowing Plan, which is normally included in the Medium-term Debt Strategy, was not mentioned as being submitted to parliament. This should not have occurred. These documents should have been readily available for public scrutiny. It is important to assess these documents along with the budget statement as they contain data and other critical information on the budget and Government medium term economic strategy. The submission of the Report of the Director of Audit for 2020 to Parliament was also needed to close the budget process for 2020.

The existence of the state of emergency and the cumulative decline in GDP of approximately nine percent between 2020 and 2021, facilitated the suspension of the fiscal rules and targets in the Fiscal Responsibility Act for the third consecutive year. The Order to suspend sections 7 and 8 of the Act was presented to Parliament and the Recovery Plan Memorandum was submitted. The Covid-19 environment has now become normal for the economy. Therefore, the fundamental issue of whether the Fiscal Responsibility Act, in its current construct, is fit for purpose needs to be addressed.

The Economic and Social Context of the 2022 National Budget

The budget statement provided information on the economic and social developments in Grenada, but more focus was needed on the social developments. The inclusion of a comprehensive assessment of the social situation was important as prior to the Pandemic there were already signs of vulnerabilities in the economy. This was evident in the rate of unemployment particularly among the youth. The IMF Article IV Report of July 2019 placed the unemployment rate at 21.7 percent in 2018 and reported that youth unemployment was high. The Pandemic exposed some other social misalignments in the economy which need direct intervention by assessing the developments in the labour market and in the social sectors particularly education and health.

In relation to the labour market, when compared with the national unemployment rate, a higher rate of unemployment was recorded for youths and women. Based on data from the Statistics Department, by the end of the 4th quarter of 2019 and 2020, the overall unemployment rate stood at 15.1 percent and 18.5 percent respectively. By the second quarter of 2021, as outlined in the budget speech, the unemployment rate was 16.6%. However, in the interest of obtaining a more comprehensive picture of unemployment, reporting on unemployment by age and sex would have been most appropriate in the context of providing targeted interventions. Specifically, in 2019, unemployment among the youth stood at 29.6 percent. By 2020, unemployment among the youths was 39.5 percent and at the end of the 2nd quarter of 2021, youth unemployment was 38.6 percent, signaling high levels of chronic youth unemployment. Also, unemployment rates for women, were higher than the national rates, accounting for 18.3% (2019), 21.6 % (2020) and 19.5 % (2021). Detailed reporting on the structure of unemployment and persons who have dropped out of the labour force was necessary for targeted government intervention.

The unemployment rate provides only a partial indicator of the welfare of the population. This must be combined with indicators of poverty. The budget statement reported a poverty rate of 25 percent for 2018/2019, based on a poverty assessment undertaken by the World Bank and the Statistics Department. Similarly, information on the structure of poverty was required to determine the welfare of the population. Along with the overall poverty rate, the Report indicated that extreme poverty increased, and income inequalities widened. Detailed information on poverty and living conditions was needed to target policies and programmes.

The social conditions and the economic situation, among other things, would have influenced the effectiveness of the approach to teaching during the Pandemic. Information needed to be provided on the impact of the virtual method of teaching. Some children are lagging in their education, and some have dropped out of the school system. This could be attributable, in part, to the lack of access to internet service, interruptions in the internet service, the unavailability of electronic devices, the unsuitable learning and living environment, and inadequate technological and advisory support. There is evidence of the ill effects of the approaches to teaching during the Pandemic. A commentary on a UNICEF Report indicated that COVID-19 has further widened the education gaps between rich and poor families in Latin America and the Caribbean, and that many of the most vulnerable students may not return to school. A situational analysis needed to be undertaken for Grenada so that Government intervention could be well targeted.

A broad coverage of health indicators should have been included in the assessment of developments in the economy. The crisis began as a health issue, and although it turned into an economic crisis, it remains a major health challenge. The health implications were not restricted to the Covid-19 virus, but it affected other aspects of health both physical and mental. There were other social dislocations that accompanied the Pandemic as persons adopted to a new way of life. Deep analysis of the current health situation and the health infrastructure was needed to inform policy directives.

The economic situation aggravated these vulnerabilities. Grenada's economy, like the other countries in the ECCU, fell over a cliff in 2020 and remained trapped in the valley in 2021. After declining by 13.8 percent in 2020, economic growth in 2021 was estimated at 4.8 percent. The slow rate of economic recovery is occurring in an inflationary period thereby suppressing real income and adversely affecting vulnerable groups.

The budget outturn in 2021 was more favourable than budgeted, recording a current surplus of $91.8M [excluding budgetary support of$37.2M] compared with the budgeted $23.9M. This was due to the higher than budgeted current revenue and lower than budgeted current expenditure. Capital spending accelerated during the second half of the year to amount to a reported $261.7M for 2021. The capital projects were financed with 'grants' of $195.4M of which $152.7M was from the National Transformation Fund.

The Estimates of Revenue and Expenditure is the Official record of government financial transaction and serves as the historical records. It is necessary to improve the document for accountability and transparency by broadening the data coverage by including a five-years series comprising two years of actual data prior to the year of the budget, the year of the budget, and projections for the two years after the budget. There should also be consistency in the data format throughout the Estimates of Revenue and Expenditure. This would avoid situations as occurred where the WRB transaction, which is a significant financial transaction, is omitted from any of the Estimates of Revenue and Expenditure.

In summary, the 2022 National Budget should have presented a more comprehensive review of social developments in 2020 and 2021. The Pandemic aggravated existing social vulnerabilities and created other social challenges. It is in this context that, Part 2, would examine the budget proposals for 2022, and their implications for the economy.

Analysis of the 2022 Budget – Part 2

It is in the context of the negative social impact of the Pandemic and the slow rate of economic recovery that this article, Part 2, examines the budget proposals for 2022 and their implications for the economy.

In the 2022 Budget, the objective of economic expansion is pursued through higher expenditure, and some tax relief. Both current and capital expenditures are budgeted to increase in 2022. In this regard, capital expenditure is budgeted at $333.8 M, compared with actual expenditure of $261.7M in 2021. The higher capital spending is combined with increased current or operational expenditure. Actual operational expenditure was $598.6M in 2021 compared to $661.7M budgeted for 2022. The allocations for all categories of operational expenditure were budgeted to increase in 2022.

Tax relief was granted through the following measures: i. The price per gallon for gasoline and diesel was fixed at $15.00; ii. the threshold for the application of VAT and the environmental levy for domestic consumers of electricity was raised to 500 kWh together with a 25 percent reduction in the non-fuel cost per kWh for all users; and iii. expansion of the list of zero-rated goods for VAT to include saltfish, turkey parts, vegetable cooking oil, cheddar cheese and split peas. These zero-rated products supplemented the existing list which, according to the budget speech, were items such as rice, flour, sugar, bread, ground provision, vegetables, and fish. These measures should bring some relief to households and other economic agents. At the macro-level, tax relief measures are intended to increase national output through higher disposable income and a corresponding increase in spending.

An important feature of the Budget for 2022 is the inclusion of the financing component. This is a good step as it facilitates fiscal transparency and allows for the examination of the financing of government operations and the impact of this on the public debt. However, this financing component would need to be examined and recalibrated to ensure consistency with international standards and with the information provided in the Estimates of Revenue and Expenditure. This is important as the financing of government operations has implications for the growth in public debt, particularly if available financial resources are not sufficient to fund the budget and for principal debt repayment. This is in the context of increased debt obligations. Based on information derived from the Quarterly Debt Bulletin of the Ministry of Finance as at September 2021, the total public debt was $2.6 billion or 88.4 percent of GDP, comprising Central Government debt of $2.1 billion or 70.7 percent of GDP and the debt of State-owned Enterprises of $527.9M or 17.7 percent of GDP, leading to issues of debt sustainability.

Implications of the Budget Proposals

The revenue measures could be considered as providing needed relief to economic agents due to the high prices at a time when incomes were constant or falling. During the period of rising prices, consumers would have adjusted their purchases or dip into their savings to maintain a level of consumption. With the relief measures, economic agents could now rebalance their budget. This is particularly so for the relief on the cost of electricity which would benefit some consumers.

The adjustment to the price of gas at the pump, while providing relief, also seems to be an attempt to align the price of gas in Grenada with the other Caribbean countries. There should not have been a pricing system where the price per gallon of gas of $17.23 in Grenada is the highest in the ECCU. Gasoline price in Grenada diverges significantly from the other countries in the ECCU, where the prices converge to approximately $14 to $15 per gallon. Operating in a common market and a single financial space, it would be appropriate for a common approach to the pricing of gas be adopted among the governments of the ECCU.

The intention of zero-rating goods is generally to ensure essential items remain affordable to low-income households. Given the socio-economic conditions, consideration should also have been given to reducing the tax burden on the poor. The report on poverty indicated that, despite the decline in overall poverty between 2008/2009 and 2018/2019, extreme poverty increased, and income inequality widened. There were more poor women headed households, and the poor families had twice the number of children compared with the non-poor families. The Pandemic would have worsened the poverty situation. The zero-rating of goods for VAT should have been targeted to a broader basket of necessities to cater for the vulnerable groups.

The higher government expenditures, combined with the tax relief measures, should contribute to economic growth and reduced unemployment. These outcomes are highly dependent on the quality of expenditure undertaken. The persistent high unemployment among youths and women and the pockets of extreme poverty need well designed programmes to elevate them out of their deprived conditions. Priority needed to be given to developing productive industries that can earn foreign exchange or save on the use of foreign exchange and provide sustainable employment. In the absence of a clearly defined strategy for building domestic productive activities, increased government expenditure would be channeled into imports at the expense of developing local productive capacity. The future growth and development of the economy would be constrained.

The quantity, quality and the focus of capital spending will determine the impact of the Budget on the economy and whether meaningful economic transformation is being pursued. It could be challenging to achieve the budgeted capital expenditure of \$333.8 M which is dependent on adequate human and financial resources.

Given the impact of the Pandemic, the capital budget must be examined in terms of its contribution to transforming the economy. Direct government intervention to transform the economy is inadequate, particularly in the agriculture, livestock, and fishing sectors and in the processing of these products. Specifically, there is still the need to develop a modern and technology driven agricultural sector and agro-processing to attract youths and that could employ women, both of whom are above the national rate of unemployment.

The operational expenditure or current account is examined in the context of its responsiveness to the Covid-19 environment. For example, in education, many students have fallen behind or dropped out of school due to the electronic form of teaching. Therefore, programmes for direct intervention targeted at recovering the lost students and remedial actions for the lagging students should have been included in the Budget. Failure to reverse this situation would have long-term consequences not only for the human capacity of the country, but also for the social fabric of the society. Such programmes, along with the reorientation of the education system, should be a component of the Covid-19 Response Project.

Priority needed to be given to upgrading the health infrastructure, including health education, community health services, mental health services and hospital services. These would need to be addressed overtime.

In reorienting government operational expenditure, there is the need for well-defined programmes for supporting a more diversified economy and for enhancing the skills of the youths so they could be integrated into the labour-force. Some of the areas previously identified for the diversification of the economy are culture, web design, data analysis and other creative and innovative industries and these would require technical, financial, and administrative support. This reorientation of government operational expenditure was observed in St Kitts and Nevis where a Ministry of Entrepreneurship, Entertainment and Talent Development was established in 2020 to develop and transform the creative and innovative industries. The Ministry provides technical and administrative support to these industries to enhance the quality of creative and innovative talent and output; and to professionalize the arts, entertainment, creative and innovation industries. This is an example of a conscious policy decision to diversify the economy by providing support to the emerging industries. This level of coherence and a strategic approach are not apparent in the 2022 National Budget.

The revenue measures would provide needed financial relief to economic agents, and government expenditure should contribute to economic growth in 2022. While it is impossible to transform the economy within one year, some structural changes should have been observed in the current and capital accounts as indicators that the government was pursuing a transformative agenda. This urgent restructuring of the economy was not a dominant feature of the National Budget for 2022.

The National Debt

The National Debt Dilemma – Part 1

A high national debt will be a legacy of the Covid-19 induced recession. In Grenada, similar to the other countries of the Eastern Caribbean Currency Union (ECCU), the steep decline in Gross Domestic Product (GDP) and the accompanying deterioration of the government's fiscal performance will result in a higher national debt.

The extent of the expected decline in economic activity can be gleaned from the assessment in the International Monetary Fund (IMF) October 2020 World Economic Outlook. In this report, the global economy is projected to contract by 4.4 percent in 2020, with the main trading partners of the ECCU, the USA contracting by 4.3 percent, the UK by 9.9 percent and Canada by 7.2 percent.

In this global context, the ECCU is forecasted to decline by 16 percent in 2020. The Grenada economy, which is highly dependent on tourism, is projected to contract by 12.2 percent. Higher national debt will be an outcome of this recession.

The debt dynamics during the financial and economic crisis of 2008 is instructive. Total public sector debt of the combined governments of the ECCU increased from 73.9 percent of GDP in 2007 to 78.8 percent of GDP in 2010. Grenada's national debt increased from 86.5 percent of GDP to 95.4 percent of GDP over that same period. A combination of debt restructuring, economic growth and improved fiscal performance contributed to a decline in the debt to GDP ratio commencing in 2014.

The Covid-19 induced recession will push countries to debt levels that are considered unsustainable. Grenada will need to contain the growth in public sector debt to avoid high and unsustainable debt.

Grenada's total public sector debt was reported at $1.89 billion or 57.7 percent of GDP in 2019. [2]The decline in GDP of 12.2 percent in 2020 and the acquisition of new debt pushed the debt to GDP ratio to 68.6 percent in 2020, equivalent to a debt of $1.94 billion. It was reported that with a projected economic growth of 6 percent, the total public sector debt is expected to be 65.7 percent of GDP in 2021, which is equivalent to $1.99 billion. The debt to GDP ratio is projected to further decline to 62.7 percent of GDP in 2023 which would be equivalent to $2.14 billion. The trend in the debt to GDP ratio will depend on the rate of contracting of new debt and the pace of economic recovery.

Grenada's Medium-term Fiscal Framework is based on the steady decline in the debt to GDP ratio from the 65.7 percent in 2021 to 62.7 percent in 2023. This is in the context of the restoration of the Fiscal Responsibility Act and the implementation of the Recovery Plan Memorandum in 2022. The decline in the debt to GDP ratio is expected to be achieved by a reduction in both recurrent and capital expenditure. Following the expansionary fiscal policy position in 2021, a more contractionary fiscal policy position will be adopted for 2022 and 2023 as outlined in the Medium-term Fiscal Framework. In 2023, recurrent expenditure is projected to decline from 19.5 percent of GDP to 16.3 percent of GDP. Capital

---

2   The public debt information is obtained from the reports of the Government of Grenada. It refers to Central Government debt. The total public debt is, at a minimum, ten (10) percent of GDP higher than central Government debt and includes the debt of State-owned Enterprises

expenditure is projected to contract from 7 percent of GDP in 2022 to 5.6 percent of GDP in 2023.

The projection for the debt to GDP ratio is based on a rapid reduction in expenditure and sustained economic growth. The fiscal risks are high, and if materialized, could hinder the achievement of the projected debt to GDP ratio of 62.7 percent by 2023. Additionally, the treatment of the settlement of the Grenada Electricity Company (GRENLEC) matter and the loan with the EXIM Bank of the Peoples Republic of China for the upgrade of the Maurice Bishop International Airport has the potential of pushing the debt to GDP ratio to more than 70 percent. Along with the debt to GDP ratio, the servicing of the debt must be considered.

With the contraction in domestic revenue, the capacity to repay debt was reduced. In the 2021 Budget, debt payments, comprising interest and principal payments, were estimated at 55 percent of recurrent revenue. Debt servicing is estimated to be 50 percent of recurrent revenue in 2022 and 48 percent in 2023. The national debt needs to be carefully managed to avoid high and unsustainable debt. At this stage, the focus should be on ensuring the efficiency and effectiveness of all government expenditures and a strategic approach to the management of the national debt.

Consequently, it is important to implement the institutional arrangements for the management of the public debt as outlined in the Debt Management Act (The Act). The underlying principle of the Act is for a systematic approach to the contracting of debt and the management of the debt. The Debt Management Act makes provisions for a Public Debt Coordinating Committee, chaired by the Permanent Secretary of the Ministry of Finance and consisting of the Head of the Budget Department; the Head of the Debt Management Unit; the Head of the Policy Unit; the Accountant General or his or her designate; a representative of the Attorney-General; and a representative of the Public Sector Investment Programme. Among its functions, the Public Debt Coordinating Committee is required to consider proposals for the assumption of new debt obligations and review the annual public sector borrowing plans. The Committee is expected to meet at least monthly and to report to the Minister of Finance. The Debt Management Unit is supposed to provide technical and administrative support to the Public Debt Coordinating Committee.

The functions of the Debt Management Unit are comprehensively outlined in the Debt Management Act. Under the supervision of the Minister, the Debt Management Unit is required to rigorously examine debt to be contracted, monitor the public debt, and advise on debt developments. The Unit is expected to prepare reports on the implementation of the Debt Management Strategy for the approval of Cabinet within one month of the end of the quarter. These technical processes are stipulated to ensure efficiency in the contraction and management of the national debt.

The Debt Management Act also makes provision for transparency in the management of the national debt. It requires the submission of a Medium-term Debt Management Strategy to Parliament at least two months before the beginning of the fiscal year; and the submission of an annual borrowing plan and a public debt management report to Parliament at the time of the presentation of the annual Budget. The Act also makes provisions for reporting on the national debt. Under the Act, (Subsection 24) states *"The Minister shall cause to be maintained and published on a website of the Government in a timely basis, accurate records of outstanding debt, guarantees, and lending transactions."* The Act further requires the publication of a statistical debt bulletin periodically.

In this high debt environment, effective debt management is critical. It is therefore necessary to adhere to the provisions of the Debt Management Act for the effective management of the national debt and for improving fiscal transparency.

The National Debt Dilemma – Part 2

With a public debt, as derived from the Debt Report from the Ministry of Finance, of approximately 2.6 billion dollars or 85.4 percent of GDP, the issue of debt sustainability should be coming to the forefront. The public debt is approaching levels that are comparable to that recorded during the 2008 to 2010 financial and economic crisis. In the post pandemic period, the nature, composition, and status of the public debt would become a national issue.

The public debt, which is generally referred to as the national debt, is an outcome of the Governments' fiscal operations. A fiscal deficit is financed by either borrowed funds or the utilization of past savings. In Grenada, the financing of the budget deficit, which includes principal debt repayment, is generally by borrowing. This fiscal outcome impacts on the public debt.

The term national debt is used as the debt is a liability of the population. The repayment of the debt is from the collection of domestic revenues and could place a financial burden on the present and future population. Therefore, the proceeds of loans should be channeled into productive economic and social activities which will facilitate the achievement of economic growth.

The public debt is considered so important that it, along with pension payments, is specifically mentioned in the Constitution. Subsection 81 (1) stipulates that all debt charges for which Grenada is liable shall be a charge on the Consolidated Fund. The Constitution defines debt as all instruments that will be liabilities of the Government. It states at 81(2) that debt charges include interest sinking fund charges, the repayment or amortization of debt and all expenditure in connection with the raising of loans on the security of the Consolidated Fund and the service and redemption of the debt created thereby.

The public debt comprises the debt of Central Government and Government guaranteed debt; the debt of public sector institutions that are established by an Act of Parliament namely statutory bodies and state-owned enterprises; and other debts that are liabilities of the Government.

This broad definition of public debt is recognized in the Public Finance Management Act (2015). The term public debt is also used in the Debt Management Act (2015) and the Fiscal Responsibility Act (2015). This is the consistency that is required of legislation. However, reports on financial management now need to be consistent with the legislation and the Constitution. This is so since a common feature of the public debt reports is the restriction of the data and analysis to Central Government debt. The reports need to provide comprehensive information on the debt of statutory bodies, state-owned enterprises and other obligations that are charges on the Consolidated Fund or obligations that are guaranteed by the Central Government.

The 2020 Economic Review and Medium-term Outlook, which presented debt data as at the end of September 2020, was restricted to Central Government debt. The debt of the state-owned enterprises was excluded from the Report. There was no reference to debt of Statutory Bodies. The Debt Management Strategy and the Medium-term Fiscal Framework for 2021 to 2023 are restricted to Central Government debt.

The omission of comprehensive information on the debt of statutory bodies, state-owned enterprises and other liabilities of the Government could lead to an underestimation of the public sector debt and the debt to GDP ratio. The public debt of 2.6 billion dollars or 85.4 percent of GDP is derived from the reported debt of Central Government and state-owned enterprises. A closure of the information gap would lead to precision in reporting on the public debt.

The Debt Report for the first quarter of 2021 placed the Central Government debt at 2.1billion dollars or 67.2 percent of GDP. The non-traditional debt of Government financial obligations to individuals for Court awarded judgement were not included in the reports. These judgement debts which are charges on the Consolidated Fund are constantly increasing due to the accumulation of interest payments. During the period that the judgement debt remains unsettled the debt burden on the population will be increasing. This rising debt burden is not efficient and hence it is not desirable, particularly in this depressed economic environment.

The debt of state-owned enterprises, based on data in September 2020, was recorded at 512.9 million dollars or 18.2 percent of GDP. Timely and comprehensive data on the operations of the State-owned Enterprises is required for the accurate reporting on the debt of these enterprises. Based on the reported Central Government debt and that of state-owned enterprises, the total public sector debt was estimated at approximately 2.6 billion dollars or 85.4 percent of GDP. There was no reference to statutory bodies.

The report indicated that there was a growth in the public debt in 2020 and in the first quarter of 2021. The higher debt was due mainly to the disbursement of loans for financing emergency expenditures associated with Covid-19. In addition, during the first quarter of 2021, there were disbursements to the Central Government from the loan from the EXIM Bank of China for the St. George's Airport Runway and Road Upgrade and Rehabilitation Project. The disbursement of loans already contracted is expected to continue and, with the sluggish economy, the public debt and debt to GDP ratio are likely to further increase during 2021.

The lack of comprehensive data presents a challenge in analyzing governments' fiscal operations and, in this case the public debt. The Debt Report seems to suggest that the Central Government is the entity responsible for contracting the debt from the EXMIN Bank of China for the St. George's Airport Runway and Road Upgrade and Rehabilitation Project. This is deduced as the disbursement from the loan was included in the analysis of Central Government debt. Improved data coverage and further disaggregation of the debt data are required to determine the holders of the public debt.

The legislative requirements are in place to facilitate the improved coverage of the public debt. The Public Finance Management Act Subsections 73 and 74 requires these bodies to submit reports to Parliament and the Director of Audit. The Act states:

73. The Minister shall present a statement of the over-all performance of all, and each Statutory Body and State-owned enterprise based on audited financial statements for the preceding year to Parliament alongside the budget proposals for the following financial year.

74. The Board of Directors of every Statutory Body shall cause to be prepared the annual financial statements of such entity and shall no later than three months from the end of the fiscal year, submit such accounts to the Director of Audit for auditing, with a copy to the line minister, and the Minister.

Ideally, reports on fiscal performance should cover the total public sector, that is, the preparation of a consolidated public sector report. The public debt should cover the debt of Central Government, statutory bodies, state-owned enterprises, Government guaranteed debt and other financial obligations of the Government. This will be consistent with the intent of the Public Finance Management Act, the Debt Management Act, and the Fiscal Responsibility Act. It will also be incompliance with the Audit Act and the role of the Director of Audit to report on the public accounts. This will support fiscal transparency which requires the publication of timely, accurate and comprehensive information.

Repurchasing of WRB Shares in Grenada Electricity Company (Grenlec)

The repurchase of WRB shares in GRENLEC by the Government of Grenada has derailed the 2020 National Budget and has the potential to derail the 2021 National Budget.

On 2nd December 2020 detailed information was presented to Parliament on the provisional outcomes of the 2020 Budget relative to the approved Budget, the 2021 Budget with the estimated expenditure for 2021, and the sources of financing the expenditure. The information is expected to be accurate and presented with integrity for the approval of Parliament.

The revelation by WRB, on 24th December 2020 of the repurchase of its shares by the Government was followed by public disclosure of this by the Government on 29th December 2020. The public was informed that the repurchase of WRB shares in GRENLEC was financed by savings on the capital account of the 2020 Budget. Subsequently, it was argued that this transaction settled a debt in response to a court judgement, and therefore was not subject to Parliamentary approval.

The transaction involving the repurchase of the WRB shares needs to be clarified. The statements by the government to date on the matter, rather than explaining the transaction to the public in clear, unambiguous terms, have generated much confusion and many questions concerning the legality of the transaction, the source of its funding and of course the impact on the Budget.

The treatment of the transaction relating to the repurchase of the shares from WRB by the Government raises the issue of the integrity of the information provided to Parliament and by extension the public. Fundamental questions arise as to

(i) whether undertaking such transaction was in compliance with the legal requirements for incurring such expenditure by the Government; (ii) whether savings were available in the capital account to finance this transaction; and (iii) whether the financial resources budgeted in the 2020 Budget could accommodate the transaction. This transaction needs to be examined in the context of the legislative framework for the budget process and the projected budget outcomes. This article examines each of these.

Legal Basis of Transaction

Fundamental to the preparation and execution of the Budget is the adherence to the provisions of the Constitution which supersedes any other legislation. The claim that the repurchase of the WRB shares for approximately one hundred and seventy million dollars ($170M) was accommodated in the 2020 Budget needs to be critically examined. Unless there was explicit provision in the 2020 Budget for this transaction, this is not legally possible based on the Constitution. There was no provision in the 2020 Budget for such an expenditure and therefore the presentation of a Supplementary Appropriation Bill to Parliament for this purpose would have been required. The Constitution specifically states that the approved Appropriation Bill is for expenditure for specific purposes. The expenditures for the specific purposes are detailed in the Estimates of Revenue and Expenditure which is presented to Parliament with the Appropriation Bill. The governance arrangements for fiscal management are outlined in sub-sections 75-79 of the Constitution.

The classification of the transaction as a judgement debt does not exempt the process from Parliamentary scrutiny and approval. The Public Finance Management Act (PFM) 2015 authorizes the Minister to settle claims against the government out of the Consolidated Fund on the advice of the Attorney General, the Accountant General and the Director of Audit, but it states clearly at Article 42 (2) that no payments shall be made out of the Consolidated Fund for claims against the government that is in excess of amounts available **in the appropriation for the purpose**. The qualification at Article 42(2) means that payment out of the Consolidated Fund to settle judgement claims against the government is only permissible if the amounts had been approved/appropriated by Parliament and secondly the amount of the claim settled cannot exceed the approved amount. Neither the Constitution nor the PFM Act makes any provision for judgement claims against the government to be settled out of any unused balances in other votes and without reverting to Parliament.

The only constitutional arrangement for expenditure not approved by Parliament is under the Contingencies Fund. The use of the Contingencies Fund is restricted to unforeseen expenditures and must be immediately followed by a Supplementary Appropriation Bill to Parliament and the Fund must be replenished.

Financing of the Repurchase of WRB Shares

The source of financing for the WRB repurchased shares also has to be interrogated. In the Government Press Conference of 30th December 2020, it was stated that the transaction was not financed from loans or grants but from savings on the capital account, described as financial resources that became available as a result of the non-implementation of capital projects in the 2020 Budget.

The failure to implement capital projects cannot be considered savings. Savings on the capital account, as commonly understood, would only accrue if projects were efficiently implemented so that the actual expenditure was less than the budgeted amount for the projects. Further it is assumed that unless these projects are cancelled, they will be implemented in 2021 and therefore the financing is still needed. It is comparable to a private investor whose construction activity was delayed due to bad weather and the unavailability of labour. The funds not spent due to the delay in implementation cannot be considered savings. In any event, resources approved by Parliament for one purpose cannot simply be appropriated for another purpose. Without following the legislated procedures, such expenditure would be unauthorized expenditure.

Another pertinent issue is the adequacy of resources in the 2020 Budget to accommodate the transaction. The 2020 Budget made provision for capital expenditure of $225M, but actual expenditure was estimated at only $122M. These capital projects were expected to be financed with capital grants totaling $201M; with $146M from the National Transformation Fund (NTF) and $55M from donors and other sources. However, only $98M in grants, of which $86M came from the NTF, was applied to capital projects in 2020 resulting in unused grant funds of $103M. It is important to note, however, that unused donor resources are not available to be diverted to other purposes without approval. Therefore, the Government only had discretion over the unused grant resources from the NTF of $60M (that is, $146M minus $86M). The resulting financial resources available due to the slow rate of implementation of capital projects should not be described as savings. The transaction is best described as a diversion of funds earmarked for capital projects to repurchase the WRB shares.

Budgetary Implications of WRB Repurchase Transaction

The fiscal performance in 2020 did not allow the Consolidated Fund to accommodate such a transaction. The information presented to Parliament on 2nd December 2020 revealed a very tight fiscal position. The financing requirement, inclusive of principal debt repayment was $237M and hence the need to borrow to finance the 2020 Budget. With such a weak fiscal position, the repurchase transaction could not have been accommodated in the 2020 Budget and would have had to be financed through another legally established fund. The most obvious would be the National Transformation Fund which is the main source of finance for capital projects.

Given this major financial transaction, an updated report on the fiscal performance for 2020 should be presented to Parliament as the repurchase transaction has derailed the Budget. A Supplementary Appropriation Bill should accompany this to regularize the expenditure. In the updated fiscal report, the following would need to be adjusted to reflect the WRB repurchase transaction: the capital grants reported on 2nd December 2020 would need to be increased by the amount used for the repurchase transaction (that is, $170M); total grants would now stand at $285M, comprising the reported grants of $115M plus $170M used for the repurchase transaction; and capital expenditure increased to $292M comprising capital projects of $122M and repurchase of shares totaling $170M. All other financial transactions associated with the repurchase of the shares would also need to be included in the fiscal performance report for 2020. The financial transaction will not affect economic indicators such as GDP and employment in 2020 as it is simply an exchange of shares without any capital investment.

The developments in 2020 will have implications for the 2021 Budget. The Budget was presented with significant risks to the outturn, including shocks affecting GDP, the persistence of the Covid-19 pandemic and less than budgeted financial inflows. The materialization of these risks could significantly alter the performance of the 2021 Budget.

The risks associated with the lower than budgeted inflows are heightened. The 2021 Budget estimates capital expenditure at $305M to be financed by grants of $244M of which $172M is from the National Transformation Fund. With the allocation of $170M for the repurchase of WRB shares, the risk of inadequate resources to finance the capital programme is real. The effect of economic shocks and the Covid-19 pandemic are risks that will continue to impact the Budget. With the emergence of the Covid-19 cluster in December and the accompanying restrictions, the economic decline for 2020 is likely to be steeper than the projected 12.2 percent. The extension of the Covid-19 concerns into 2021 over the peak tourism season will dampen economic activity. In this Covid-19 environment, economic recovery will be slow and achieving the projected 6 percent growth in 2021 would be a challenge. The derailing of the Budget implies higher national debt.

In this volatile and challenging environment, public policy decisions should concur with legislative requirements, be transparent and based on sound technical advice. The public should be continuously engaged, and this should be supported by the publication of timely, regular, comprehensive, and easy to understand reports.

Grenlec Transaction Exposes Blind Spot in National Budgets

Sunday 24th January 2021 will be one month since the revelation by WRB of the repurchase of its shares in GRENLEC by the Government of Grenada. The population is still perplexed, despite the statements by government ministers and in Parliament. The main areas of contention remain the legality of the transaction and the source of funds for the repurchase of the shares.

The information provided on the source of funds to repurchase the shares in GRENLEC is ambiguous and is one of the main causes of the confusion. In the Government Press Conference on 30th December 2020, the public was informed that the repurchase transaction was financed, not by loans or grants, but by savings on the capital account and from savings accumulated from 2013. The savings on the capital account was explained to be the result of the low rate of implementation of the capital budget. In its Press Release on 12th January 2021, an alternative report on the financing of the repurchase transaction was given. The public was informed that the transaction was financed by grants and concessionary loans from the 2020 Budget. At the sitting of Parliament on 15th January 2021, the nation was informed that the repurchase transaction was financed by savings on the capital account of the 2020 Budget.

Although there have been public pronouncements, citizens remain perplexed. The complexities of identifying the source of financing are combined with the lack of Parliamentary approval for the expenditure as required by the Constitution. In addition, the available funds in the approved Budget for 2020 was not sufficient to finance the repurchase transaction;

and so, the question of where the funds came from remains unanswered.

This ongoing debate has brought to the forefront some blind spots in the Budget which need to be resolved. These blind spots call into question the accuracy, consistency and comprehensiveness of the information presented to Parliament; and the consistency and application of the legislation that informs the budget process. The outcome of these blind spots is a systemic failure of the financial management system, including the operation of the checks and balances for protecting the integrity of the public accounts.

Currently, a thorough assessment of the Government financial position is impossible due to the lack of information on all Government financial transactions. This is brought about by, among other things, the failure of the Government to publicly disclose detailed information on the performance of the National Transformation Fund through which most of the capital projects in the Budget are financed.

In 2020, seventy (70) percent or $86m of the $122m in capital projects was financed from the National Transformation Fund. It is projected that $172m will be withdrawn from the National Transformation Fund to finance the estimated $305m in capital projects in 2021. The lack of transparency in the operation of the National Transformation Fund is a major cause of the confusion on the financing of the repurchase of the WRB shares in GRENLEC. It is a blind spot in the Budget which inhibits a thorough assessment of the financial position of the Government and complicates the tracing of the financing of the repurchase of the WRB shares.

This is specifically related to the ambiguous use of the word grants as a source of financing of the national Budget. In the Budget documents two types of grants could be identified.

There are official grants from governments, institutions, and agencies such as China, the Caribbean Development Bank (CDB) and the European Development Fund (EDF) and these are itemized in the Budget documents. Generally, the Government does not have discretion on the use of these funds which account for a small proportion of capital expenditure. The official grants were estimated to be $29m or twenty-four (24) percent of the $122m of capital expenditure in 2020.

The other type of grants referred to in the Budget documents are grants from the National Transformation Fund. The Citizen by Investment Act (2013) makes provisions for successful applicants to make investments or contributions to approved capital projects. These investments or contributions by the Economic Citizens are deposited in the National Transformation Fund and are defined as external grants. These 'grants,' which are presented to Parliament as a total amount, were budgeted at $172m in the 2021 Budget as previously indicated. These are different from official grants and the ambiguous use of the word 'grants' has contributed to the confusion on the financing of the capital projects.

Most importantly, the investments or contributions to approved projects by Economic Citizens should not be classified as capital grants but as capital receipts. The payment is a requirement for the purchase of citizenship and therefore is a component of the cost of acquiring Grenadian citizenship. In contrast, a grant is a gift. It is a transfer not linked to an exchange for a good, service or asset. It is non quid pro quo. Consequently, the classification of the public accounts, particularly the financing of the capital account, would need to be revisited.

As such, for transparency, the public information on the use of grants, particularly for the contentious WRB repurchase transaction, should differentiate between the official grant inflows and 'grants' defined by the Government as those received from Economic Citizens through the National Transformation Fund. To declare publicly that the repurchase transaction was not financed by grants or loans and to inform subsequently that it was financed by grants and concessionary loans is confusing and does not lend itself to fiscal transparency. The announcement of the financing of the repurchase transaction by concessionary loans was a new phenomenon that added further complexities to the financing of the repurchase of the WRB shares. The information presented in Parliament did not address the fundamental cause of the confusion among the population, one of which, is the blind spot in the Budget, that is, the National Transformation Fund. Accordingly, the reports on the fiscal performance presented to Parliament do not accurately reflect Government's financial position.

The non-disclosure of information on the National Transformation Fund is contrary to the intent of financial management as envisaged in the Constitution and the Public Finance Management Act (2015). The Constitution, subsections 75 and 76 makes provision for the establishment of the Consolidated Fund and other Funds established by Acts of Parliament. This is reinforced by the Public Finance Management Act which in subsection 45 makes provision for the establishment of Special Funds as approved by Parliament. The National Transformation Fund is one such Fund, established by an Act of Parliament to receive inflows from the Citizen by Investment Programme. Along with the proceeds from the sale of citizenship, the Citizen by Investment Act makes provision for a component of the inflows to be investment or contributions to approved projects. These provisions in the Citizen by Investment Act, which were approved by Parliament, have significant implications for the management of the public finances. In the system of good government, the

Executive (Cabinet) is accountable to the Parliament. Therefore, Parliament should receive comprehensive reports on the operation of the National Transformation Fund and any other Funds established by an Act of Parliament. Reporting on the National Transformation Fund should be an integral part of the Budget. To omit reports on the National Transformation Fund undermines the creditability of the Budget. This questions the comprehensiveness and hence the accuracy of the information; and the degree to which the Executive (Cabinet) has been accountable to the Parliament.

The original intent of the legislation was for the operation of the Citizen by Investment Programme and the National Transformation Fund to be transparent. The Citizen by Investment Act (2013) Subsections 14 and 15 provided for the public disclosure of information. The existence of the blind spot in the Budget due to the non-disclosure of information on the National Transformation Fund, and the accompanying lack of fiscal transparency, point to the need to reactivate the information disclosure requirement. The non-disclosure of information from the National Transformation Fund and the exclusion of this information from the reports presented to Parliament could compromise the financial management system and the checks and balances for protecting the integrity of the system.

The Public Finance Management Act and the Audit Act, which operationalize the provisions of the Constitution, provide standards for maintaining the integrity of the public accounts. It is the responsibility of the senior officers of the Ministry of Finance to advise the Executive (The Cabinet) on financial matters. Specifically, the Accountant General has to ensure that all expenditures were duly authorized and accurate and comprehensive records are maintained of the public accounts. The Public Finance Act elaborates on the components of the public accounts to include the Consolidated Fund and Special Funds. The Accountant General is also obligated to submit the public accounts to the Director of Audit. It is the responsibility of the Director of Audit to report to Parliament, through the Minister of Finance on the public accounts. Finally, the Public Accounts Committee has the parliamentary responsibility to examine the public accounts and report to Parliament. It is doubtful whether these requirements for efficient financial management were implemented as reports on the National Transformation Fund were not presented to Parliament.

Ensuring accountability and transparency in budgeting is the responsibility of all economic agents with the support of Non-Government Organizations. It is also imperative that international and regional institutions that undertake surveillance of the economy provide comprehensive reports on the public finances which will support the principle of fiscal transparency.

Grenada's Constitution: Parliamentary Approval and the Grenlec Transaction

It is common knowledge that the purchase of the WRB shares in GRENLEC by the Government of Grenada occurred without Parliamentary approval. However, during the debates on the legality of the repurchase transaction, it was publicly pronounced that the transaction conformed with all legislative requirements. This article highlights the legislative requirements for effecting such transactions and explores whether the repurchase transaction conformed with the legislative requirements.

The provisions for financial management are embedded in the Constitution which is the supreme law of the land. All Acts of Parliament must be in conformity with the Constitution. The Public Finance Management Act gives practical effect to the constitutional provisions for financial management. To strengthen financial management and introduce fiscal discipline, Parliament approved the Public Finance Management Act (2015), the Debt Management Act (2015) and the Fiscal Responsibility Act (2015). The Audit Act remained in effect for ensuring accountability of the Executive to Parliament. For effective public financial management, all the relevant Acts of Parliament must be consistent with each other and most importantly with the Constitution. Financial management practices must also comply with the legislation.

In the sitting of Parliament on 15th January 2021, the repurchase transaction was described by the Government as a judgement debt; and was therefore not subjected to Parliamentary approval. The pronouncement in Parliament did not comprehensively, and hence accurately, reflect the full provisions of subsection 42 of the Public Finance Management Act. Subsection 42(2) is equally relevant. As explained in a previous article "GRENLEC Transaction Derails National Budget":

*"The classification of the transaction as a judgement debt does not exempt the process from Parliamentary scrutiny and approval. The Public Finance Management Act (PFM) 2015 authorizes the Minister to settle claims against the government out of the Consolidated Fund on the advice of the Attorney General, the Accountant General and the Director of Audit, but it states clearly at Article 42 (2) that no payments shall be made out of the Consolidated Fund for claims against the government that is in excess of amounts available **in the appropriation for the purpose**. The qualification at Article 42(2) means that payment out of the Consolidated Fund to settle judgement claims against the government is only permissible if the amounts had been approved/appropriated by Parliament and secondly the amount of the claim settled cannot exceed the approved amount."*

The WRB transaction clearly does not meet the conditions set out in Subsection 42 (2).

At this point, it is important to examine the legislative provisions governing public expenditure and the reallocation of funds in the Budget. As stipulated by the Constitution, the Executive must seek Parliamentary approval for all expenditures for the fiscal year through the Annual Appropriation Bill. It is recognized that the need for unplanned expenditure may arise during the implementation of the budget. This occurs because the budget is a forecast and developments in the economy could differ from what was forecasted. There could be human errors during the preparation of the budget or the emergence of unforeseen events. The Constitution makes provision for Parliamentary approval of expenditures not included in the annual Appropriation Bill through provisions for Supplementary Appropriation and Contingencies. This ensures that there is Parliamentary approval for all expenditures. It is therefore clear that the repurchase of the WRB shares which was not covered by any of the provisions governing public expenditure in the Constitution, did not have Parliamentary approval.

The Government explained that the WRB repurchase transaction was made possible by the reallocation of savings from the capital account in the 2020 Budget. While uncertainties persist on the availability of savings in the capital budget, the reallocation of funds must be guided by the relevant legislation.

It is understandable that the Executive (Cabinet) needs a degree of flexibility in the management of the approved budget. This flexibility is achieved through granting the Executive the authority to transfer and reallocate funds. This is an international practice with countries adopting different approaches. The fundamental principles that inform the transfer and reallocation of funds are that such adjustments should not undermine the credibility of the budget and the authority of Parliament. This is achieved through an integrated and comprehensive legislative and regulatory framework. In this context the reallocation of funds in the budget to undertake the WRB repurchase transaction is examined for conformity with the legislative provisions.

In Grenada, the transfer and reallocation of funds in the national budget are governed by subsections 36 and 37 of the Public Finance Management Act (2015). Subsection 36 provides for the virement of funds, that is, the transfer of funds among programmes within Votes and among Votes as follows:

36.—(1) "Subject to subsection (2), if, in the opinion of the Accountable Officer, the exigencies of the service render it necessary or expedient to vary the amount assigned to any programme within an expenditure vote as shown in the annual or supplementary estimates of expenditure for a financial year, the Accountable Officer may, subject to any order of the Minister under subsection (3), direct by means of a virement warrant under the Accountable Officer's hand, that savings arising from an item in an expenditure vote contained in the annual or supplementary estimates approved by an Appropriation Act or a Supplementary Appropriation Act be applied in aid of another item in the expenditure vote contained in the annual or supplementary estimates if the amount of the appropriation in the vote is not thereby exceeded.

Subsection 36 is not applicable to the repurchase transaction as it specifically states that these expenditures must be within Votes and must be approved by an Appropriation Bill or Supplementary Appropriation Bill.

Subsection 37 of the Public Finance Management Act makes provision for the reallocation of funds from approved budget, but this is less precise and not written with clarity and seems to be in conflict with the provisions of the Constitution. According to subsection 37(1):

"Subject to subsection (2), the Minister may by means of a reallocation warrant under the Minister's hand, direct the Accountant General that savings arising from an expenditure vote approved by an Appropriation Act or a Supplementary Appropriation Act be applied in aid of any item in any other expenditure vote in those estimates or **in aid of any new item of expenditure and the amounts to be applied shall be deemed to have been appropriated for that purpose.**"

The lack of clarity is associated with the term *"or in aid of any new item of expenditure and the amounts to be applied shall be deemed to have been appropriated for that purpose."*

If new expenditure here means that funds can be allocated to expenditure not approved by Parliament, this undermines the credibility of the budget and the efficiency of financial management and is in direct conflict with the Constitution. The accountability of the Executive to Parliament will be completely eroded. In situations of ambiguity in the interpretation of laws and conflict between Acts of Parliament and the Constitution, the Constitution prevails.

A review of the WRB transaction in the context of the legislative framework governing public financial management in Grenada leads to the conclusion that (1) the manner in which the WRB transaction was effected cannot stand up to scrutiny under Subsections 42 (1) and 42(2) of the Public Finance Management Act which makes provisions for settling judgement debts; (2) it was not approved by Parliament as part of the Annual Appropriation Bill , Supplementary or Contingency expenditure as provided for in the Constitution; and (3) any application of Subsection 37 of the Public Finance Management Act for the reallocation of approved funds to purposes unauthorized by Parliament will be in direct conflict with the provisions of the Constitution. It must be noted that even if compliance with the Public Finance Management Act was achieved, the Executive (Cabinet) has an obligation to ensure that the provisions conform with the Constitution. The Attorney General, as the legal adviser, provides such assurance to the Executive (Cabinet). In all decisions, the Constitution is always supreme.

It is important that all Acts of Parliament are clear and precise and conform with the Constitution. This will allow for efficient public financial management and transparent fiscal policy.

Fiscal Summary Leaves WRB Transaction an Unsolved Mystery

The Government has released its Fiscal Summary report for December 2020. This report published on the Government website, https://www.finance.gd/index.php/fiscal-reports, has not shed much light on the financing of the repurchase of the WRB shares in GRENLEC.

In the fiscal table provided, capital expenditure for December 2020 was reported at $178.5M. It is obvious from the size of the reported capital expenditure for December 2020 that elements of the WRB repurchase transaction were included. In this situation, ideally, the capital expenditure should have been disaggregated into expenditure on capital projects and the purchase of shares. This precision in the fiscal summary table would have allowed the public to be better informed about the WRB transaction.

The Fiscal Summary report is inconsistent with official statements on the source of the funds for the WRB transaction. Hence, the financing of the repurchase of the WRB shares in GRENLEC by the Government of Grenada remains a mystery. The positions of the Government as pronounced by Ministers, on various occasions, were: (i) the transaction was financed by savings accumulated due to prudent fiscal management from 2013; (ii) savings from the 2020 capital budget due to the non-implementation of capital projects; and (iii) from grants and concessionary loan. Until comprehensive reports on Government finances are presented to the public, the WRB financial transaction will remain an unsolved mystery.

In the Fiscal Summary report, despite a large capital expenditure of $178.5M, the grants reported as spent in December was only $13.6M. This amount of grants ($13.6M) was far below the approximately $170M required to finance the WRB transaction. The figures in the Fiscal Summary for December 2020, failed to show that the expenditure for the WRB transaction was financed by grants. This conclusion is further corroborated by an examination of the full year data for 2020 as presented in the Fiscal Summary report.

For 2020, the Government spent $103.1M in grants. This presumably consisted of budgetary support, along with capital grants as defined by the Government, which contributed to financing the $269.9M in capital expenditure. It can therefore be deduced that this large capital expenditure included amounts for the WRB transaction. The grants expended were significantly below the required amount for the repurchase of the WRB shares. It is clear that the grants allocated to capital projects that were not implemented in 2020 were insufficient and was not utilized to finance the WRB transaction.

Based on this examination of the Fiscal Summary report for December 2020, it could be concluded that the WRB transaction was not financed by grants or from savings on the capital budget for 2020. By this process of elimination, the WRB transaction mystery is gradually unfolding.

It is impossible to accurately determine, from the Fiscal Summary report for December 2020, the financing of the WRB transaction as the information provided in the summary table is incomplete. The table showed that the Government needed, at least, $147.8M to close the revenue/expenditure gap for December 2020. When the full year of Government operations is considered, the Government needed to find $128.1M to finance its operations.

The Fiscal Summary did not provide any information on where the Government obtained the funds to finance this deficit. This is a serious omission in the reporting on Government finances. It makes it impossible to determine the financing of Government operations and, in this case, the WRB transaction from an examination of the Fiscal Summary report as published by the Ministry of Finance. The audited public sector accounts which should be presented to Parliament in October 2021 may provide information that could solve the mystery of the WRB financial transaction.

In going forward, the publication of the various reports by the Government should not only be seen as meeting its statutory obligations but should be regarded as an opportunity to educate the public about the business of government through presentation of easily understood and complete information and analyses in these reports.

Transparency and Accountability in Government Finances

It is the sixth month of the 2021 fiscal year and the financing for the repurchase of the WRB shares in GRENLEC by the Government of Grenada remains a mystery. The lack of comprehensive fiscal reports inhibits assessment of government's financial operations, and in this case, the financing of the WRB transaction.

The Government informed, on various occasions, that the sources of financing the WRB repurchase transaction were savings, grants, and concessionary loans. The Fiscal Summary Report for December 2020 and the Debt Reports for 2020 and the first quarter of 2021, as published by the Ministry of Finance, did not provide any information that would allow for the identification of the sources of financing for the WRB financial transaction.

In the previous article on this subject, the conclusion was that the WRB transaction was not financed by 'grants.' With 'grants' eliminated as a source of financing, there are two other options for the financing of the WRB transaction: borrowings, and/or the utilization of accumulated savings as stated by the Government. An assessment of whether the repurchase was financed by loan is now undertaken, by an examination of the use of loans to finance the 2020 budget gap.

The financing gap arose as grants ($103.1M) and the surplus on the current or operational account ($38.8M) were insufficient to finance the abnormally high capital expenditure of $269.9M. Specifically, there was an overall budget deficit of $128M for 2020. This deficit does not take into account principal debt repayment of $190.9M for 2020. The principal debt repayment taken together with the overall budget deficit resulted in an estimated overall financing gap (budget gap) of approximately $319M for 2020. This meant new resources had to be found to cover this financing gap.

In general, a financing gap can be closed through additional borrowings (from domestic and/or external sources), use of reserves or through the accumulation of arrears. The omission of the financing component in the Fiscal Summary Report meant that no information was provided on the source(s) of financing to close the budget gap.

However, based on the information in the quarterly Debt Reports, it was estimated that new loan disbursements totaled $176.1M in 2020 which partially closed the financing (budget) gap leaving the sum of $142.5M still to be financed (See Table). In the absence of the financing component in the Fiscal Summary Report, the additional source(s) of funds for financing the 2020 budget cannot be determined.

Financing for the 2020 Budget

	Item	EC$ Mn.
1	Total Grants	103.1
2	Current Account Balance	38.8
3	**Available to Finance Capital Expenditure (1 +2)**	**141.9**
4	Total Capital Expenditure	269.6
5	**Overall Balance (3 – 4)**	**-127.7**
6	Principal Repayment	-190.9
7	**Financing gap (5 + 6)**	**-318.6**
8	**Financing Required**	**318.6**
9	Disbursements	-176.1
10	Unidentified Financing (8 – 9)	142.5

Calculated from Fiscal Summary December 2020 and Debt Reports for 2020 published by Ministry of Finance

Although money is fungible, the Debt Reports from the Ministry of Finance did not indicate whether any of the loans received by the Government of Grenada in 2020 was used to repurchase the GRENLEC shares. In fact, these loan funds were mainly (78%) from multilateral institutions for managing the Covid-19 Pandemic. Specifically, the Government received approximately $60.5M from the International Monetary Fund (IMF), $54.3M from the International Development Association (IDA) and $29.9M from the Caribbean Development Bank (CDB). The Debt Report for the fourth quarter of 2020, the period during which the WRB transaction occurred, showed loan disbursements to the Central Government of only $13.7M. Clearly, this was far less than the amount required for the financing of the WRB transaction.

Similarly, the Debt Report for the first quarter of 2021 did not attribute any of the $127.9M in new loan disbursements to the WRB financial transaction. This debt was associated with disbursements for emergencies arising from the Covid-19 Pandemic and for the St. Georges Road and Airport Upgrade Rehabilitation project.

As at the end of March 2021, the various publicly available Debt Reports from the Ministry of Finance have not attributed any new loan disbursements to the repurchase of the WRB shares in GRENLEC by the Government of Grenada. This provides another partial insight to the financing of the WRB transaction. If the Debt Reports from the Ministry of Finance comprehensively capture Central Government's debt transactions, the repurchase of the WRB shares in GRENLEC by the Government of Grenada was not financed by loans.

The reports published by the Ministry of Finance are incomplete to allow for a thorough analysis of the state of the government finances. As indicated, the inclusion of the financing component in the Fiscal Summary Report is necessary to determine how the budget gap for 2020 was closed. The sources of financing need to be explicitly stated in the reports. It is only through the publication of comprehensive public sector accounts that the financing of the 2020 Budget, and by extension, the repurchase of the WRB shares in GRENLEC by the Government of Grenada would be unraveled.

In keeping with the legislative and administrative requirements for the publication of the public accounts, comprehensive information for 2020 should be available by October 2021. The Accountant General is required to submit the public accounts for 2020 to the Director of Audit by June 30, 2021, and the Director of Audit is then obligated to submit the public accounts to Parliament for review, through the Minister of Finance in October 2021. Fiscal reports should include information on the source of financing for the budget gap for 2020.

Until timely, accurate and comprehensive reports on Government finances are presented to the public, fiscal transparency is compromised, and the WRB financial transaction would remain an unsolved mystery.

Government Finances

On the celebration of the 47th anniversary of Independence, on Sunday 7th February 2021, Prime Minister Dr. Rt. Hon. Keith Mitchell unveiled a suggestion for the establishment of a Social Fund (The Fund). This announcement has led to many queries about the operational aspects of the Fund.

This has compounded ongoing debates on national issues, with no firm closure, holding the population in constant abeyance. At the end of 2020, the repurchase of the WRB shares in GRENLEC by the Government evoked many discussions. In January, it was the non-payment of the agreed four (4) percent salary increase to public officers which remains unresolved. In February, the issue of the Social Fund was added to the mix.

Uncertainties about the Social Fund have arisen because of the failure of the Government to return to the public with information on the nature of the Fund, its management, and operational features. The nation was given a brief introduction to the proposed Social Fund. The need for the Fund was attributed to the continuing impact of the Covid-19 pandemic and the accompanying loss of income for a wide cross-section of the population. The objective of the Fund is to provide income support to those in the population who are hurting due to the Covid-19 pandemic.

It was explained that the Fund will not be established by an Act of Parliament and that it will be financed by voluntary contributions from members of Cabinet and from the working population. The amount of the individual contribution to the Fund will not be defined but will be determined by the contributors based on "their conscience in the context of a Christian society." The proposal was in search of a creative way of raising financial resources to provide income support to the unemployed and for addressing the plight of the poor and vulnerable.

It is not new for innovative mechanisms for addressing economic and social conditions to emerge, particularly during crisis. There are many examples from past experiences during which innovative ideas evolved to address urgent economic and social issues. The depression of the 1930's, characterized by declining economic activity and high unemployment, was a turning point for approaches to addressing the impact of economic recessions. Prior to the depression, it was advocated that government should not be deeply involved in the economy. However, to address the economic and social ills of the 1930's, the economic thought that emerged argued that government should play a greater role, by increasing its expenditure, to stimulate economic growth and reduce unemployment.

A watershed period for the Caribbean was the 1940's to the 1970's when economic and social conditions were depressed. The economic thought, at that time, championed government intervention in the economy and the transformation of the economic and social structures, by the generation of adequate capital and the development of systems to direct the capital to economic and socially deserving areas. This approach to the transformation of the economic and social structures was guided by different political philosophy. This was vividly manifested by the contrasting strategies of the Grenada United Labour Party Government and that of the People's Revolutionary Government.

Innovative ideas to address economic and social dislocations in the past placed a great responsibility on government. This pandemic is unprecedented and requires deep thinking on the models for the development of the economy to allow for sustainable growth, thereby reducing the chronic unemployment and poverty. The pandemic has shown that the thinking underlying the existing model for development needs revamping. It is hoped that a new trend of economic thought will emerge from this crisis.

A Social Fund, while it may provide short term relief to some of the affected, will not address the root causes of unemployment and poverty. The implementation of the Fund to provide support to the unemployed and the poor and vulnerable will be confronted with complexities that need to be resolved before implementation.

The Social Fund, which will not be established by an Act of Parliament, will be outside the realm of the national budget and will not be a direct fiscal policy instrument. The Fund will be a private programme. Therefore, the expenditures from the Fund cannot be defined as government expenditures as all government expenditures must be approved by an Act of Parliament.

Additionally, the contributions from individuals will not be public funds as all government revenues must be deposited in the Consolidated Fund or Special Funds established by an Act of Parliament. Statutory bodies and state-owned enterprises, which are public bodies, are all governed by Acts of Parliament and therefore were not intended to be used to establish the Fund. In the absence of these governance structures for the establishment of the Social Fund, it will be a non-government or private Fund.

As a result, public officials will have no legal authority for the management of the Fund. Specifically, the Accountant General will not be responsible for recording the transactions of the Fund. The Director of Audit will not be required to audit the account and report to Parliament. The Fund will be outside the remit of the Public Accounts Committee. There will be no Parliamentary oversight.

Accountability for the Fund will be determined by the governance structure of the Fund if such is established. In this situation, the contributors to the Fund would be required to be knowledgeable of the laws and regulations that will govern the operation of the Fund. The population that are not acquainted with the legislation will be disadvantaged as they will not have the protection of Parliamentary oversight, as in the case of public funds.

As a private Fund, there will be options for its establishment. It could be implemented through the operations of a private entity that is generally established and governed by the Company's Act. These private companies are governed by a Board of Directors and a managerial staff. Alternatively, the Fund could be operated by the establishment of a 'Not for Profit' organization. In this case, the process will need to be subjected to the registration and accompanying requirements for approval. The management and operation of the Fund will be governed by rules and regulations that are applicable to NGO's and guidelines as determined by the collective agreement of the contributors to the Fund. The establishment of the Fund, under either of these governance structure, has cost implications and the Fund should only be implemented after a cost benefit analysis has been undertaken.

The objective of the Fund fits in the category of government core responsibility, particularly in this time of recession. It is targeted at assisting the population who are unemployed or suffered from reduction in earnings due to Covid-19. It is seeking to redistribute income from the employed to assist persons that are unemployed or do not have adequate income. While non-government organizations could assist, this is a core function of government that it should implement through its taxing and spending policies. The redistribution of income, particularly during a recession, will not be effective through a private venture. The Government should take full command for comprehensively addressing the economic and social situation. This function should never be outsourced.

Also, a system of voluntary contributions, which is based on one's conscience, is not a sustainable mechanism for financing government activity and particularly the social dislocation caused by Covid-19. The financial contributions will be unpredictable while a reliable and steady flow of funds is needed to provide the income and employment support. The government is expected to manage this redistribution of income in society by its authority to raise revenue or seek financial resources and to channel these resources to the deserving economic and social areas. The public is kept informed of the efficiency or inefficiency of this redistribution through the approval and monitoring of the budget by Parliament.

The redistribution of income from the employed to the unemployed and other vulnerable groups raises the issues of equity or fairness of the economic system. The notion of equity or fairness must be supported by societal consensus. Therefore, transparency in the operation of income redistribution programmes, which includes social safety net programmes, is required. A comprehensive and accurate system of personal information is needed for the proper targeting of the beneficiaries. This must be accompanied by a robust system for the distribution of benefits. This redistributive responsibility of the government, which requires some societal consensus, should be subjected to Parliamentary oversight.

Closure to budgetary issues could only be achieved by dialogue and consultations based on timely, accurate and comprehensive information and analysis. Consequently, clarity and precision should be applied to the Social Fund which involves the redistribution of income from the employed to the unemployed and other vulnerable groups. This will facilitate fiscal transparency which is a component of good governance. At this time, deep and critical thinking is required to transform the economy based on a sustainable model of development.

Government Finances and the Economy – Part 1

Grenada's ailing economy could ill afford the impact of the ongoing dispute on the capacity of the Government to pay salary increases to public officers. In the final analysis, the economic and social cost of the dispute will far outweigh the estimated $13M to be paid to public officers. The controversy arose as the Government reneged on its signed Agreement to pay the four (4) percent salary increase. A more effective approach would have been through consultation with the view of achieving a 'Win-Win' outcome and arriving at a mutual agreement. At this junction, real dialogue based on publicly available up-to-date, accurate and comprehensive information should be the starting point for dialogue and resolving the dispute.

Importantly, the monitoring of the performance of the economy and the National Budget, and the publication of the accompanying reports to the public are critical in this 'low or no growth' and volatile economic environment. These reports should provide a comprehensive assessment of the financial position of the Government.

There are two major gaps in the published fiscal data. The financing component of the accounts needs to be included in the published reports. It provides information on either the sources of funds to finance a deficit or the allocation of resources derived from a surplus. Additionally, the operational summary of the National Transformation Fund and the transactions with the Consolidated Fund should be presented with clarity.

Notwithstanding these gaps, this Article, Part 1 is an analysis of the fiscal performance for 2020, based on the revised fiscal data published on the Ministry of Finance website www.finance.gd. Following the publication of the first quarter data, Part 2, would be the review of fiscal developments in the first quarter of 2021.

The information presented to Parliament on 2nd December 2020 were preliminary estimates of the performance of the economy and government finances. The revised data published for 2020 is the starting point in the analysis of government finances and the economy for 2021.

The developments in December 2020 made the information provided to Parliament redundant. In that month, there was the emergence of the Covid-19 cluster and the accompanying restrictive measures which had a negative impact on the economy. Therefore, the estimated decline in GDP of 12.6 percent as reported then would need to be revisited to determine the actual performance of the economy in 2020.

Then there was the repurchase of the WRB shares in GREN-LEC by the Government for a reported one hundred and seventy million EC dollars ($170M). This transaction affected fiscal developments in 2020, as according to the Government, the repurchase transaction was financed by 'grants' and concessionary loans derived from savings in the capital account of the 2020 Budget.

In 2020, the financial position of the Government tightened. This was due in part to the adverse impact of the Covid-19 Pandemic on domestic revenues and the shortfall in 'grants'. This lower than projected financial inflows were combined with the higher than budgeted expenditure. Operational or current expenditure was marginally higher than budgeted as the Government responded to the demands of the Covid-19 Pandemic. However, capital expenditure unexpectedly surpassed the budget as it included the repurchase of the WRB shares in GRENLEC. The higher than budgeted expenditure combined with the weak domestic revenue performance tightened the Government finances.

The actual data for 2020, as published by the Ministry of Finance, showed that operational or current revenue of $689.6M was 12 percent or $96.6M less than the budgeted amount of $786.2m. The impact of the Covid-19 recession was also manifested in the revenue performance relative to 2019. The revenue collected in 2020 was $88.4M or 11 percent less than that collected in 2019.

However, expenditure, both current and capital, exceeded the budgeted amount and was higher than the amount incurred in 2019. Current or operational expenditure of $650.8M was $16.8M or 2.8 percent more than the budgeted amount of $634M. The comparison of current expenditure with 2019 showed that the current or operational expenditure for 2020 was $27.3M or 4 percent more than the amount spent in 2019. The revenue and expenditure performance in 2020 resulted in a surplus on Government current or operational account of $38.8M. This was significantly lower than the budgeted surplus of $152.2M and the actual current account surplus of $154.5M in 2019.

Developments on the capital account further tightened the volatile fiscal position. Capital expenditure for 2020 was $269.9M, which surpassed the budgeted $225M. This higher than budgeted expenditure included the repurchase of the WRB shares in GRENLEC. The surplus of $38M on the current account and the use of 'grants' were not sufficient to finance the capital expenditure. The Government spent $103.1M in grants compared with the budgeted 'grants' of $218.6M. The shortfall in 'grants' combined with the higher than budgeted expenditure contributed to a widening of the fiscal imbalances.

Consequently, the Government recorded a primary deficit of $72.3M and an overall deficit of $128.1M in 2020. This overall deficit does not include principal debt repayment which would increase the funds required to close the revenue/expenditure gap in the 2020 Budget.

Information on the financing of the deficit in 2020 is not publicly available. This is because the financing component of the account is not included in the published fiscal reports. The omission of the financing of Government operations needs to be corrected as fiscal transparency requires the publication of timely, accurate and comprehensive information.

Government Finances and the Economy – Part 2

Fiscal policy, as the main instrument of economic management is the business of all citizens. In Grenada, fiscal policy is implemented through the execution of the annual national budget. The preparation, implementation and evaluation of the budget should be participatory. For effective consultation and dialogue, information on the policies, outcomes, and their impact should be presented with clarity and precision.

The Government publishes monthly data on the fiscal performance on the Ministry of Finance website www.finance.gd.com; and the monthly fiscal summary tables for the months of January to May 2021 have been published. The coverage of the data has gradually improved over the period to include principal debt repayments and loan disbursements. This is a step on a path to improving fiscal transparency.

However, there is a fundamental deviation from the standard practice for fiscal reports. Each monthly report needs to include a summary of the year-to-date financial position of the government as at the date of the published report. Currently, to assess the state of the government finances over a period, the data in each of the individually published monthly fiscal report must be aggregated. This practice inhibits persons who do not have the time, energy, and technical knowledge to consolidate the monthly reports from assessing the state of the government finances. Also, an accompanying analysis of the data, including the rationale for deviation from the expected or the normal trend, would be of great benefit to the citizens.

The important section of the report, that is, the financing component remains outstanding and could only be partially constructed based on published data. The Fiscal Summary

Reports include data, in memo form, on the National Transformation Fund. In the absence of a summary report, the interpretation of the status of the Fund is left to the citizens. Timely, accurate and comprehensive publicly available data, along with easy-to understand reports, is a perquisite to real dialogue.

Notwithstanding these challenges, the following is an analysis of the fiscal performance for the first quarter of 2021 based on an aggregation of the monthly Fiscal Summary Reports from the Ministry of Finance for January, February, and March. This aggregated monthly data for the first quarter of 2021 showed that the Government recorded (i) a current account surplus of $27M; (ii) a primary surplus of $36.7M; and (iii) an overall surplus of $16.3M inclusive of principal debt repayment of $12.5M. Based on the Debt Report published by the Ministry of Finance, the government finances were boosted during the first quarter by the receipt of $127.9M in loan disbursements. The overall surplus of $16.3M, combined with the loan disbursement of $127.9M, resulted in available financial resources of $144.2M as at the end of March 2021.

Current or operational revenue of $176.3M was 2.6 percent or $4.5M more than the $171.8M government projected to collect in the first quarter of 2021. The details on the categories of revenue that contributed to the higher revenue yield was not provided in the report. It is therefore impossible to pronounce on any contributing factors.

In comparison, the revenue performance for the first quarter of 2021 was weaker than the first quarter of 2020. This was expected as economic activity was more robust during the first quarter of 2020. The impact of the Covid-19 pandemic began to be manifested in March 2020 and intensified thereafter. The first quarter of 2020 was therefore a relatively normal year for economic activity and government finances.

In contrast, the first quarter of 2021 experienced weaker economic activity as the Covid-19 pandemic persisted. In particular, the continued collapse of the tourism industry; and the absence of residential students at the St Georges University impacted negatively on the hotels and restaurant sector. The effects are generally pervasive throughout the economy with negative impact on transportation, communication, utilities (electricity and water) and the wholesale and retail trade.

Consequently, the comparison with 2020 showed that the current revenue collected in the first quarter of 2021 was $ 29.5M or 14.3 percent less than that collected in the first quarter of 2020. This was due to lower tax revenue particularly revenue from the expenditure related taxes, that is, taxes on goods and services and international trade. It therefore reflected reduced expenditure in the economy which is generally consistent with a sluggish level of economic activity.

While current revenue performed better than projected, current expenditure outpaced the amount the government allocated for the period. Current or operational expenditure was $149.3M for the first quarter of 2021. This was higher than the Government's projected expenditure of $146M for that quarter. This was due to higher than planned expenditure on goods and services. All the other components of current expenditure were within the amount projected to be spent during the quarter. When compared with 2020, current or operational expenditure in the first quarter of 2021 was $6.2M less than the expenditure of $ 155.5M incurred in the first quarter of 2020. The lower current expenditure in 2021 was due to a reduction in transfers and subsidies as government spent $35.2M for the first quarter in 2021 compared to $47.1M for the same period in 2020.

With these developments, the Government realized the current account surplus of $27M for the first quarter of 2021.

This surplus was higher than the $25.8M that the Government planned to achieve for the quarter. However, it was lower than the current account surplus of $50.3M achieved in 2020.

Government investment during the first quarter, as reported on the capital account, was less than planned. However, there was more capital spending in the first quarter of 2021 compared with the first quarter of 2020. During the first quarter of 2021, capital expenditure of $23.4M, was significantly less than the planned capital spending of $65.1M. Correspondingly, lower 'grants' of $25.4M was recorded compared with the planned utilization of $57M in 'grants.' The capital expenditure of $23.4M in the first quarter of 2021 was $8M more than was spent during the first quarter of 2020.

Implementation of the capital budget appeared to be challenging. At the end of the first quarter, capital expenditure was 7.7 percent of the budgeted amount. The capital budget for 2021 will need to be re-examined as significant capital expenditure would be required for the remainder of the year to achieve the budgeted $305M.

With these developments on the current and capital accounts, the government recorded a primary surplus of $ 36.7M and an overall surplus of $ 28.8M for the first quarter of 2021. These balances were higher than the primary surplus of $25.9M and overall surplus of $17.7M that the Government planned to achieve in the first quarter of 2021. However, they were lower than the fiscal balances in 2020 when the primary surplus was $63.9M and the overall surplus was $56M. The following table is a summary of the government's finances for the first quarter as derived from the monthly Fiscal Reports:

Central Government Finances EC$M

Government Finances	Targeted 2021	Actual 2021	Actual 2020
Total Revenue and Grants	228.7	201.6	226.9
Grants	57	25.4	21
Current Revenue	171.8	176.3	205.8
Total Expenditure	211	172.8	170.9
Current Expenditure	146	149.3	155.5
Capital Expenditure	65.1	23.4	15.4
Current Account Balance	25.8	27	50.3
Primary Balance (After Grants)	25.9	36.7	63.9
Overall Balance (After Grants)	17.7	28.8	56

Source: Derived from the monthly fiscal report of the Ministry
of Finance for January, February and March 2021.

The loan disbursement of $127.9M during the first quarter boosted the financial resources available to the government. The overall surplus of $28.8M was reduced to $16.3M due to principal debt repayment of 12.5M. The overall surplus of $16.3M and the loan funds of $127.9M resulted in available funds of $144.2M at the end of the quarter. Further analysis of the finances is constrained by the lack of publicly available information.

Comprehensive information on the public finances would be available to the public when the Mid-year Fiscal Policy Report is presented to Parliament in keeping with Subsection 25 of the Public Finance Management Act (2015). It is anticipated that the Mid-year Fiscal Policy Report would be timely, with accurate and comprehensive information; and easy to understand analysis. In so doing, it will be consistent with the principles of fiscal transparency.

Government Finances and the Economy – Part 3

The monitoring of the National Budget and reporting on its outcomes are important components of the budgetary process. A review of the Governments' finances for the first six months of 2021, showed that the fiscal performance was mixed. The outturn on the current or operational account was stronger than projected; while capital expenditure was less than planned. This assessment was based on the monthly Fiscal Summary Reports for January to June 2021 as published on the Ministry of Finance website www.finance.gd.com.

Government Finances and the Economy – Part 2, outlined the challenges of using the monthly Fiscal Summary Reports to assess the current state of the public finances. There is a fundamental deviation in these fiscal reports from the standard practice for reporting on fiscal performance. The monthly reports do not include a 'year-to-date' position. Therefore, to assess the state of the government finances over a period, the data in each of the individually published monthly fiscal report must be aggregated. This practice should be rectified as it compromises fiscal transparency. To reiterate, it inhibits persons who do not have the time, energy, and technical knowledge to consolidate the monthly reports from assessing the state of the government finances.

The following is an analysis of the fiscal performance for the first six months of 2021 based on an aggregation of the monthly Fiscal Summary Reports for January to June. The aggregated monthly data for the first six months of 2021 showed that the Government recorded (i) a current account surplus of $34.9M; (ii) a primary surplus, after 'grants', of $60.9M; and (iii) an overall surplus, after 'grants', of $35.8M.

The current account surplus of $34.9M realized for the first six months of 2021 was above the $23.6M that the Government planned to achieve for that period. This was due to higher revenue yield when compared with the amount the Government projected to collect.

Current or operational revenue of $352.1M was 7 per cent or $23M more than the $329.1M Government projected to collect in the first six months of 2021. The details on the categories of revenue that contributed to the higher than projected revenue yield was not provided in the report. It is therefore impossible to pronounce on which category of taxes contributed to the higher than projected revenue yield. Revenue in both the first and the second quarters of 2021 was higher than projected. However, the higher revenue yield was more pronounced in the second quarter when $18.5M or 11.8 per cent more in revenue was collected than projected.

In comparison, the revenue yield of $352.1M for the first six months of 2021 was $3.1M higher than the first half of 2020. This was influenced, in part, by the extremes of economic conditions brought about by the Covid-19 pandemic. In the second quarter of 2020, the global economy, including Grenada, was in virtual lockdown and domestic economic activity would have contracted. In contrast, with the partial lifting of international and domestic restrictions, economic activity was higher in the second quarter of 2021 compared with the second quarter of 2020. Consequently, in the second quarter of 2021, current revenue particularly from expenditure related taxes, that is, taxes on goods and services and international trade and transactions were substantially higher than collected in the second quarter of 2020. This was combined with higher non-tax revenue, generally associated with fees and fines. This revenue outturn during the second quarter boosted the total revenue intake for the first six months of 2021.

While current revenue performed better than projected, current expenditure outpaced the amount the Government allocated for the period. Current or operational expenditure was $317.2M for the first six months of 2021. This was higher than the Government's projected expenditure of $305.5M for that period. The deviation was due to higher than planned expenditure on employee's compensation and goods and services.

Comparatively, the current or operational expenditure of $317.2M in the first six months of 2021 was $5.7M less than the expenditure of $322.9M incurred in the first half of 2020. The lower current expenditure in 2021 was primarily due to the reduction in transfers and subsidies as Government spent $77.6M for the first six months in 2021 compared to $98.3M for the same period in 2020. The rollout of the stimulus package would have contributed to the peak in transfers and subsidies in 2020. Thereafter, expenditure in that category would have normalised. With these developments, the Government recorded the current account surplus of $34.9M at the end of June 2021 which was higher than the surplus of $26.1M at the end of June 2020.

Government investment during the first six months, as reported on the capital account, was less than planned. Capital expenditure of $51.4M, was significantly less than the planned capital spending of $124.9M. Correspondingly, lower 'grants' of $52.5M was recorded compared with the planned utilization of $109.7M in 'grants.' However, capital spending during the first six months of 2021 was $19.1M more than the first half of 2020. Implementation of the capital budget is lagging. At the end of the first six months, capital expenditure was 17 per cent of the budgeted amount. The lagging projects have not been identified in the Fiscal Summary Reports. The capital budget for 2021 will need to be re-examined and prioritized as it is obvious that the budgeted capital expenditure of $305M would not be achieved in 2021.

Combining the current and capital operations, the Government recorded a primary surplus as derived by excluding interest payments from the overall balance. The primary surplus before 'grants' was $8.4M. With the inclusion of 'grants', the primary surplus after 'grants' was $60.9M. There was an overall deficit, before 'grants' of $16.7M and after 'grants' a surplus of $35.8M for the first six months of 2021. These balances were stronger than the primary surplus, after 'grants' of $36.1M and overall surplus, after 'grants' of $8.4M that the Government planned to achieve in the first six months of 2021. However, these were slightly higher than the fiscal balances in 2020.

The following table is a summary of the Government's finances at the end of June 2021 as derived from the monthly Fiscal Reports.

Central Government Finances EC$M

Government Finances	Targeted 2021	Actual 2021	Actual 2020
Total Revenue and Grants	438.7	404.6	386.3
Grants	109.7	52.5	37.2
Current Revenue	329.1	352.1	349
Total Expenditure	430.3	368.7	355.2
Current Expenditure	305.5	317.2	322.9
Capital Expenditure	124.9	51.4	32.3
Current Account Balance	23.6	34.9	26.1
Primary Balance (Before Grants)	-73.6	8.4	19.6
Primary Balance (After Grants)	36.1	60.9	56.8
Overall Balance (Before Grants)	-101.3	-16.7	-6
Overall Balance (After Grants)	8.4	35.8	31.2

Source: Derived from the monthly fiscal report of the
Ministry of Finance for January to June 2021.

The financing component, inclusive of debt transactions, could not have been analysed as the financing section of the fiscal account remains outstanding. This component not only informs about the sources of financing of the budget but provides the checks and balances that ensure the integrity of the fiscal accounts. This deficiency would need to be addressed.

More comprehensive information on the Government finances would be available to the public when the Mid-year Fiscal Policy Report is presented to Parliament in keeping with Subsection 25 of the Public Finance Management Act (2015).

Unravelling: Issuing Bonds to Pay Salary Arrears to Public Officers

The financing of the arrears of salaries to public officers by issuing bonds directly to them, and if in need of immediate cash, their subsequent sale of these bonds to financial institutions require examination for the implications to the Government and people of Grenada, public officers, and financial institutions.

Financing the arrears of salaries to public officers with bonds could be described as a strategy for compulsory saving and investment by public officers. They will not be receiving cash in hand, but bonds, which will earn a rate of return if these are held to maturity. While savings and investment are good for the economy, such decisions ideally should be the responsibility of the individual after assessing their personal financial situation and the cost and benefit of any financial investment.

Implications for the Government and People of Grenada

The economic and social costs of the impasse over salary arrears between the Government and public officers have not been assessed and quantified; but created a debt, which could have been avoided. With the proposal of issuing bonds to finance the arrears of salary the Government is substituting one kind of debt (arrears of salaries) with another type of debt (bonds). With this proposal, the net debt position of the Government will remain unchanged. However, the interest charges due on the bonds will accrue on the current account, adding to the Government's operational expenditure.

Ideally, the face value of the issued bonds should include interest that accumulated on the arrears of salaries to public officers. The interest rate of three (3) percent would then be applied to the face value of the bonds. Consequently, the interest accrued on the outstanding salary arrears and the interest that will have to be paid on the issued bonds are additional charges on the public purse. The timely payment of the four (4) percent salary increase could have avoided the accumulation of debt with the accompanying interest cost.

Even, in this present situation, if the arrears of salaries to public officers are financed with revenue or with 'grants,' the liability of the Government for the arrears of salaries would be eliminated without the additional interest cost associated with the bonds. In contrast, the debt, now in the form of bonds, would remain outstanding accruing interest until the bonds are redeemed.

The issue of bonds to finance the arrears of salaries due to public officers means that the Government is contracting debt to finance accumulated arrears on current operations. This is not considered prudent fiscal policy. Contracting debt to finance current operations should be used only if alternative cheaper financial resources are not available. This should not be the case in Grenada. Based on the estimated fiscal position at the end of June 2021, the Government realized a current account surplus of $34.7M. Therefore, the retroactive payment could have been financed with a portion of this surplus from the current operations instead of a new debt created through the issue of bonds. Another possible source of financing is the revenue from the sale of passports which is channeled into the National Transformation Fund. Expenditure on wages and salaries are current or operational expenses and borrowing, through the issue of bonds, to finance such expenses should be a last resort.

This borrowing, which is the bond issue, is taking place in the context of high and increasing public debt and a substantial shrink in national income. Central Government debt has risen from $1.89billion in 2019 to $1.99billion in 2020 and to a further $2.13billion by June 2021. Coupled with the decline in GDP, the debt to GDP ratio of Central Government rose from 59.9 percent in 2019 to 70.4 percent in 2020 and to 71.5 percent by June 2021. With the inclusion of the debt of State-owned Enterprises, the total public debt amounted to $2.63billion or 88.5 percent of GDP at the end of June 2021. Given the deterioration in the debt profile of the country, debt financing for operational expenditure should be a last resort.

Implications for the Public Officers

The proposal to issue bonds directly to public officers will mean that the officers do not have immediate access to cash. If in need of urgent cash before the maturity date, the officers will have to sell the bonds. In the absence of an active bond market, the public officers may need to sell the bond at a steep discount, that is, at an amount much less than the face value of the bond. As such, public officers would receive a sum of cash less than the amount of their salary arrears. The purchasers, most likely the banks and other financial institutions, would be the main beneficiaries, particularly if a high discount rate is applied to the bonds. If this occurs, it would be equivalent to transferring resources from public officers to these financial institutions. There is one caveat. If financial institutions, such as credit unions, with broad-based membership, in which public officers are members, are the purchasers of these bonds, then some of the profits earned on these discounted bonds would be returned to the members as dividends.

If the bonds are held by public officers to maturity, they will receive the full face-value as well as the accrued interest on the bonds. The financial benefits to the public officers would depend on the rate of interest applied to the bonds. The interest rate on the bonds would need to be higher than the rate of inflation with provision for a positive return on the investment after accounting for inflation. This is a global inflationary period. Grenada's inflation is mostly imported. Based on the IMF World Economic Outlook for July 2021, the rate of inflation in the USA, Grenada's main trading partner, is projected at 4 percent in 2021 and 3.2 percent in 2022. The duration of the inflationary period is uncertain, and, in any event, price levels would be higher than in 2021. The real value of money, that is, the amount of goods and services that a quantum of money could buy would be less in the future. For the public officers to receive a positive return on this savings and investment in bonds, the interest rate on the bonds would need to be higher than the increases in the general prices, as measured by the rate of inflation, with an additional margin for the return on investment. This would need to be compared with returns that can be earned on alternative investment products in Grenada.

The uncertainties of holding government debt must be factored into the decision to hold bonds. Government debt has traditionally been described as sovereign debt. This implied that the debt had minimum risk and it was safe to hold Government debt. This has changed overtime. Government debt has become risky as it has been subjected to debt restructuring involving haircuts or extension in the maturity date of the debt. Sovereign debt is no longer considered safe.

Implication for Financial Institutions

Financial institutions are likely to benefit whether the bonds are repurchased from the public officers or directly from the Government. If the bonds are issued directly to public officers and these are subsequently sold, the financial institutions stand to gain on the difference between the discounted value of the bond and the face value at maturity as well as the accrued interest on the matured bonds. In the case of a financial institution taking up the bonds directly from the Government, it will receive the face value plus the interest at maturity. In either case, it is beneficial for a financial institution with high liquidity to invest in the bonds. In a situation of high liquidity, financial institutions are holding deposits which they would prefer to lend. Interest is paid on deposits and if these are not lent, they are being held at a cost to the financial institutions. It is therefore in the interest of financial institutions with high liquidity to invest these deposits in bonds and earn interest which would partially offset the interest paid on deposits.

In summary, the debt associated with the payment of the four (4) percent salary increase to public officers should not have been created. By issuing bonds to finance the arrears of salary to public officers the Government is substituting one kind of debt (arrears of salaries) with another type of debt (bonds). The public officers could benefit from the direct issue of bonds if held to maturity and the interest rate on the bonds is higher than the rate of inflation with an additional margin for the return on investment. If officers need cash and they are forced to sell these bonds, public officers will most likely receive less than the face value of the bonds and therefore less than the salary arrears due. Financial institutions with liquidity stand to gain from purchasing the bonds which would be a source of income and possibly capital gain. Rigorous assessments of the implications of policy proposals are important in determining the best options.

The Fiscal Responsibility Act

Grenada and the tourist dependent economies of the Eastern Caribbean Currency Union (ECCU) are grappling to recover from the economic and social fallout from the Covid-19 Pandemic. During this recovery period, the Governments would depend on fiscal policy for stabilizing the economies and placing them on a path of sustainable growth and development.

In Grenada, fiscal policy is guided by the Fiscal Responsibility Act No. 29 of 2015 (The Act). This Act provides a foundation for establishing a transparent and accountable rule-based fiscal responsibility framework in Grenada. The objectives of the Act are: (a) to ensure that fiscal and financial affairs are conducted in a transparent manner; (b) to ensure full and timely disclosure and wide publication of all transactions and decisions involving public revenues and expenditures and their implications; (c) to ensure that debt is reduced to, and then maintained at a prudent and sustainable level by maintaining primary surpluses that are consistent with this object; and (d) to ensure prudent management of fiscal risks.

The Fiscal Responsibility Act was passed by Parliament on 29 May 2015 and by the Senate on 5 June 2015. In assessing the objectives of the Act consideration must be given to the economic and social environment. In the year preceding the passing of the Act the economic environment was buoyant. The international economy had recovered from the global financial and economic crisis and recorded of 3.6 percent growth in 2014. In the ECCU, the tourism industry recovered, and in most countries, there was the implementation of the Citizen by Investment Programme and the associated construction of hotels and villas. The private sector was therefore actively engaged in the economies and contributed to the economic growth of 3.8 percent in 2014.

Grenada's economy grew by 7.3 percent which reflected the growth in tourism and construction. Given the high dependence on tourism and education services, the private sector played an important role in stimulating economic growth. The improved economic activity and inflows from the Citizen by Investment Programme boosted Government finances, and with the debt restructuring, the debt to GDP ratio declined.

The economic and social landscape has changed drastically from the 2014 period. The global lockdown in 2020 due to the Covid-19 Pandemic caused a drastic shrink in global national income and unemployment soared to unprecedented levels. The social sectors, particularly education and health, were challenged. The tourist dependent economies of the ECCU were severely affected and economic activity contracted by 16 percent. Consequently, the governments assumed a more active role in the economy.

Grenada was no exception. The economy contracted by an unprecedented 12.2 percent with the accompanying growth in unemployment. Private sector activity almost ceased with the halt in tourism and the exit of the students from the St Georges University. The education sector was dislocated. Economic recovery is expected to be slow and tedious. These developments were unforeseen at the time of the crafting of the Fiscal Responsibility Act. In this environment, the Government is expected to play a significant role in economic recovery.

Even under normal economic conditions, the restrictions of the Fiscal Responsibility Act inhibit its use as a fiscal policy instrument to transform the economy. The transformation of the economy requires well targeted capital expenditure which has implications for Government primary expenditure.

Improving education and health services, even under normal economic circumstances, could, in some years, significantly increase primary expenditure on personal emolument and goods and services.

A binding annual primary expenditure rule of two (2) percent growth in real terms, limits the discretionary powers of the Government to allocate resources to meet the needs of the economy at a particular time. This discretionary power is extremely important during this recovery period when resources need to be allocated to the provision of education, health, and other social services.

The binding primary expenditure rule is also applied to capital expenditure financed from domestic resources. This affects government's ability to undertake major infrastructure projects that are financed from domestic resources. Expenditures on capital projects are lumpy and is difficult to be constrained within the binding expenditure rule of two (2) percent real growth. While fiscal rules and targets allow for fiscal discipline, they should be designed with flexibility to facilitate the use of fiscal policy to manage the economy. This is most important during this recovery period as Government addresses the economic and social impact of the Pandemic.

At this time, the fundamental issues relating to the Fiscal Responsibility Act are (i) Whether the application of the Act conforms to the tenets of accountability and transparency in fiscal policy (ii) If fiscal policy is the main instrument for economic management, is there need for amending the Act; and (iii) How appropriate is the application of the Act, in its current form, for addressing the need to restore the economy to sustainable growth.

Issues of data deficiencies, transparency, and consistency have been identified in the application of the Fiscal Responsibility

Act. These need to be addressed. In previous articles: 'Transforming the Economy with Fiscal Policy – Reforming the Fiscal Responsibility Act', areas for amending the Act to improve transparency and consistency, and as an instrument for economic development were highlighted.

Additionally, the Fiscal Responsibility Oversight Committee (FROC), in its 2019 Annual Report, indicated that recommendations for amending the Act were put forward by the International Monetary Fund (IMF). The FROC has also recommended amendments to the Act and, in its 2019 Annual Report, stated: "As it stands given the extensive amount of amendments which the FROC, MOF and IMF believe are necessary to enhance the FRA, it is the FROC'S respectful submission that the current legislation – the Fiscal Responsibility Act No. 29 of 2015 – should be repealed and replaced".

During the Covid-19 Pandemic, the expenditure rules and targets in the Fiscal Responsibility Act were rightfully suspended. In March 2020, the Escape Clause in the Act was invoked, and the expenditure rules and targets were suspended for that fiscal year. In December 2020, the suspension of the fiscal rules and targets was extended to the 2021 fiscal year. The Recovery Plan Memorandum, as required by subsection 10(4) of the Act, should have been submitted to Parliament. The Recovery Plan Memorandum is expected to set out the measures to secure compliance with the fiscal rule, target, or corrective measure and should inform fiscal policy in Grenada over the medium-term.

A reform of the Fiscal Responsibility Act is however required. In reforming the Act, the operational relationship between the Consolidated Fund and the National Transformation Fund will need to be well defined. The resources from the National Transformation Fund, defined by the Government as 'grants', are used to finance capital projects. As a source of development financing, transparency and accountability are required on the operation of the National Transformation Fund. In implementing an amended Fiscal Responsibility Act, the existing data deficiencies must be addressed. Comprehensive data on the public sector must be presented. At present, data is provided only on central government operations while the Act covers central government along with qualifying statutory bodies and state-owned enterprises. As a result of the lack of comprehensive data on the public sector, the Act is not applied as legally required.

The opportunity should now be taken by the Government to thoroughly examine the Fiscal Responsibility Act for consistency, transparency, accountability and as a policy instrument to facilitate economic development. These findings should guide the reform of the Fiscal Responsibility Act making it fit for purpose.

The Budget Alert issues remained unresolved in 2021, except for the resolution of the payment of arrears of salaries to public officers. Pension and gratuity remained a legal issue to be resolved through the Court. The establishment of the Social Fund was not pursued. The other issues notable, the purchase of the WRB shares in GRENLEC; the reforms to the Fiscal Responsibility Act; and the settlement of Court Awarded Judgement debt remained outstanding in 2021. The structure of the economy and the economic and social impact of the Covid-19 Pandemic, taking into consideration the outstanding fiscal issues, should inform budget developments in 2022.

Appendix

Appendix 1 Budget Alert

Budget Alert No.	Title of Article	Date of Publication
1	Proposals for the 2021 National Budget	November 2020
2	The National Debt Dilemma	11th November 2020
3	COVID – 19 Induced Approach to Transforming the Economy – Resetting the National Sustainable Development Plan (NSDP)	20th December 2020
4	GRENLEC Transaction Derails National Budgets	7th January 2021
5	GRENLEC Transaction Exposes Blind Spot in National Budgets	21st January 2021
6	Grenada's Constitution: Parliamentary Approval and the GRENLEC Transaction	5th February 2021
7	A peep into the Social Fund	19th February 2021
8	Fiscal Summary Leaves WRB Transaction an Unsolved Mystery	12th March 2021
9	Is the Fiscal Responsibility Act (FRA) Fit for Purpose	9th April 2021
10	Government Finances and the Economy – Part 1	8th May 2021
11	National Debt Dilemma – Part 2	22nd May 2021
12	Transparency and Accountability in Government Finances	5th June 2021
13	Government Finances and the Economy – Part 2	19th June 2021
14	Budget Alert Advisory	11th July 2021 (Not Published)
15	Government Finances and the Economy – Part 3	23rd July 2021
16	Unravelling: Issuing Bonds to Pay Arrears of Salaries to Public Officers	21st August 2021
17	Reflections on the Covid-19 Pandemic	24th September 2021
18	A Budget with a Human Touch	8th October 2021
19	Analysis of the 2022 National Budget – Part 1	10th December 2021
20	Analysis of the 2022 National Budget – Part 2	17th December 2021

The Author

Ms. Laurel Bain was formerly employed as a Senior Director at the Eastern Caribbean Central Bank. She has strong technical and administrative skills which were strengthened as she served for over 25 years in various positions including that of Deputy Director in the Research Department, Senior Director of the Statistics Department and Adviser and Senior Director in the Governor's Office.

Ms. Bain has undertaken numerous assessments of the economies of the Eastern Caribbean Currency Union (ECCU) and research on fiscal policy and taxation issues in the ECCU. Ms. Bain has worked extensively with international development agencies and regional institutions. She represented the countries of the ECCU at the IMF and the World Bank and participated in ongoing dialogue with these institutions.

Ms. Bain was engaged in capacity building programmes in CARICOM. She provided training to senior public officers in Dominica, Montserrat, Anguilla, and trainers in these countries along with The Bahamas and the Turks and Caicos Islands. She has been involved in undertaking assessment and developing training programs for parliamentarians, with Guyana as the pilot.

Ms. Bain is the Author of the books: Fiscal Policy the Economy and The Tax Structure of the Member Countries of the ECCB.

Ms. Bain holds a Bachelor of Science (BSc) and Master of Science (MSc) degrees in Economics from the University of the West Indies, St Augustine, Trinidad, and Tobago.

Contributors

The Articles benefited from the knowledge and experiences of Dr Juliet Melville, Mrs. Gemma Bain-Thomas and Ms. Renee Lewis.

Dr Juliet A Melville is an Independent Consultant and Director of Venture Research (B'dos) Inc. She has over twenty years' experience in international development work with fifteen of these at the Caribbean Development Bank where she served in various capacities including Acting Director of Economics, Chief Economist and Chief Research Economist She possesses strong skills in economic analysis, economic planning and policy formulation and was routinely involved in the monitoring and analysis of socio-economic developments in Caribbean countries and the wider international community, producing regular reports and providing strategic and operational advice. Dr Melville also led and provided technical support on high-level country missions for policy dialogue with officials on programming, projects, policy-based support, macro-economic management, and economic performance and maintained on-going policy dialogue with governments.

Dr Melville is knowledgeable and proficient in all aspects of project cycle management including project appraisal, project planning and implementation, monitoring and evaluation, risk management and procurement. She has assisted countries in designing operations aimed at improved economic governance, public sector modernization, financial sector stability, fiscal consolidation, and debt sustainability as well as poverty and vulnerability reduction.

Dr Melville is an experienced researcher and was instrumental in the establishment of the Social and Economic Research Unit at CDB. She has publications in the area of poverty, social protection, debt, structural adjustment, regional integration, and transport. She is an accomplished trainer, facilitator and teacher and has developed and delivered tertiary level training, seminars, workshops, and conferences.

Dr Melville has collaborated extensively with leading regional and international development agencies. Dr Melville was a Lecturer in Economics at the University of the West Indies (UWI) St, Augustine., and holds degrees in BSc. Economics, MSc. Economics and Ph.D. Economics.

Mrs. Gemma Bain-Thomas is an Independent Contractor. She has considerable experience in public policy and public administration; having served in a senior capacity in various ministries and departments in the Grenada Public Service for thirty (30) years. Among the senior positions held were that of Secretary to Cabinet, Permanent Secretary and Senior Administrative Officer.

During her public service career, Mrs. Bain-Thomas participated in and contributed to several public sector reform initiatives including the Value for Money studies, the training for the introduction of a new Performance Appraisal System and proposals for the regulation of private practice for medical personnel in the Public Service. She was involved in the re-organization of the Ministries of Social Development and Carriacou and Petite Martinique Affairs, the strengthening of the Cabinet Office and securing of training for senior managers of the Public Service.

Mrs. Bain-Thomas has served as a Director on the Board of Directors of several organizations and is an Accredited Director. She is the Author of the book Unconstitutionally Removed.

As an Independent Contractor, Mrs. Bain-Thomas undertook several short-term consultancies and projects which included the development of a communications and a human resource policy for local institutions.

Mrs. Bain-Thomas has attended several short-term training courses in areas of human resource development, strategic and corporate planning, and project management. She is the holder of a B.Sc. in Public Administration and Law from the University of the West Indies, Cave Hill, Barbados; an LLB from the University of Wolverhampton, London, England and an MBA in International Business from St. George's University, Grenada.

Ms. Renee Lewis is a recent university graduate and is a Research Officer on economic and management issues. She has been engaged in research on the performance of the countries of the Eastern Caribbean Currency Union (ECCU). She contributed to the coordination of workshops and conferences from 2018 to 2020 as an undergraduate at the University of the West Indies, St Augustine, Trinidad, and Tobago. These included:

Student Assistant – Conference of the Economy (COTE)

Student Assistant – Conference of the Economy (COTE) Youth Day

Student Assistant – Outreach Committee at the Department of Economics

Ms. Lewis was a member of the COTE Youth Committee in the Department of Economics, of the University of the West Indies (2018-2020).

Ms. Lewis holds a Bachelor of Science (BSc) degree in Leadership and Management with a minor in marketing from the

University of the West Indies, St Augustine, Trinidad, and Tobago.

We appreciate the comments and suggestions from all the readers of Budget alert.